The Principal's Survival Guide

Where Do I Start? How Do I Succeed? When Do I Sleep?

Susan Stone Kessler, Ed.D.
April M. Snodgrass, M.Ed.
Andrew T. Davis, Ed.D.

16pt

Copyright Page from the Original Book

Copyright © 2015 by Susan Stone Kessler, Ed.D., April M. Snodgrass, M.Ed., and Andrew T. Davis, Ed.D.

All rights reserved under International and Pan-American Copyright Conventions. Unless otherwise noted, no part of this book may be reproduced, stored in a retrieval system, or transmitted in any form or by any means, electronic, mechanical, photocopying, recording, or otherwise, without express written permission of the publisher, except for brief quotations or critical reviews. For more information, go to www.freespirit.com/permissions.

Free Spirit, Free Spirit Publishing, and associated logos are trademarks and/or registered trademarks of Free Spirit Publishing Inc. A complete listing of our logos and trademarks is available at www.freespirit.com.

Library of Congress Cataloging-in-Publication Data
Kessler, Susan Stone.
   The principal's survival guide : where do I start? how do I succeed? when do I sleep? / Susan Stone Kessler, April M. Snodgrass, Andrew T. Davis.
        1 online resource.
        Includes bibliographical references and index.
   Description based on print version record and CIP data provided by publisher; resource not viewed.

(paperback) 1. School principals—Handbooks, manuals, etc. 2. School management and organization. I. Snodgrass, April M. II. Davis, Andrew T. III. Title.
   LB2831.9
   371.2'012—dc23

2014046227

Free Spirit Publishing does not have control over or assume responsibility for author or third-party websites and their content. At the time of this book's publication, all facts and figures cited within are the most current available. All telephone numbers, addresses, and website URLs are accurate and active; all publications, organization, websites, and other resources exist as described in this book; and all have been verified as of October 2014. If you find an error or believe that a resource listed here is not as described, please contact Free Spirit Publishing. Parents, teachers, and other adults: We strongly urge you to monitor children's use of the Internet.

Edited by Eric Braun
Cover and interior design by Colleen Rollins

Free Spirit Publishing Inc.
Minneapolis, MN
(612) 338-2068
help4kids@freespirit.com
www.freespirit.com

TABLE OF CONTENTS

INTRODUCTION: Seriously, When Do I Sleep?	ii
CHAPTER ONE: Getting Started	1
CHAPTER TWO: Establishing a Vision and Goals	24
CHAPTER THREE: Policies, Practices, and Procedures	43
CHAPTER FOUR: Encouraging Teamwork and Camaraderie	103
CHAPTER FIVE: Working with New and Veteran Teachers	123
CHAPTER SIX: Supporting Teachers at Every Level	167
CHAPTER SEVEN: Leading Change	189
CHAPTER EIGHT: Documenting	211
CHAPTER NINE: Speaking the Different Languages of the Principal	236
CHAPTER TEN: Taking Care of Yourself	286
REFERENCES	311
ACKNOWLEDGMENTS	315
ABOUT THE AUTHORS	320
Index	325

This book is dedicated to our children Bradley, Daniel, Ellie, Lauren, Logan, Marit, Sarah, Wynne, and Zachary, whose existence in this world compels us to demand good teachers, good principals, and good schools.

INTRODUCTION

Seriously, When Do I Sleep?

"Be careful what you wish for. You just might get it."

You wanted to be a principal. Maybe you worked under superior leaders who inspired you to follow their example. Or maybe you worked under a bunch of goofballs who couldn't find an eraser on a chalk rail with both hands—you thought kids deserved better, and *you* are the better. However you got here, you may now feel a combination of nausea, paralysis, fear ... and excitement. It's time for you to put up or shut up, as the saying goes.

Here's the good news: You will put up. (Sometimes you may shut up, too.) You will be a great leader in some moments. In other moments, you will make not-so-great decisions in front of people who told you not to do what you did. And you will have sleepless nights.

Until you don't. Because one day the principalship will stop being terrifying. One day being a principal will seem intuitive, predictable, and even somewhat routine. One day the little things won't blossom into big things. People will trust your advice and follow your lead. One day people will believe in your ability to lead them through a difficult situation. You will lead them, and they will be glad you were there. And so will you.

You Are the Principal

This book was born out of our conference presentation, "When Do I Sleep? Surviving the Principalship." At these conferences, we have met hundreds of new and veteran principals who were drawn to the presentation because the title resonated with them regardless of how many years of experience they had. In talking with many of these enthusiastic but exhausted principals, we learned that the feeling of being overwhelmed by the job is universal—from coast to coast and from preK to high school—and we're all grateful to meet other principals who share it.

As the demands on principals have increased over the last decade, it can feel like we need to be all things to all people at all times. Some might ask, "Who would want to be a principal in this day and age?" Between school violence, helicopter parents, teen pregnancy, student drug use, high accountability, limited resources, and the easy scapegoating of educators for all societal ills, many educators think being a principal would be a terrible job.

But it isn't. Being a principal is a great job, and we know this because it's the most important job we have ever done. Schools need effective leaders. *Kids* need effective leaders.

Leading them is both deadly serious and downright fun.

This book is about how to solve the problems that occur in schools with rational logic, balanced emotion, and experience. It is written by three principals who share the goal of remaining principals. The principal job isn't a stepping stone for us. We do not aspire to be central office administrators or full-time university professors once we have mastered the principalship. We aren't headed to our state capitol to be legislators, and we aren't searching for our next gig. We have the jobs we want, and we want to keep growing as individuals and professionals. Together we have over four decades of experience in elementary, middle, and high schools as teachers, assistant principals, and principals in rural, suburban, and inner-city public schools. We have worked in large and small schools. We have been department heads, team leaders, PTO/PTA members, athletic coaches, and drama sponsors. We have been colleagues, and we have been subordinates, and among us we are parents to eight children. As parents, we have been challenged to look at leading a school not just through the eyes of the leader, but through the important eyes of the student and the parent.

What we have learned, again and again, is that for every challenge a principal faces, there are at least twice as many benefits—like working with adults who adore children. After all, true teachers almost always happen to be truly wonderful individuals, individuals who like working with and learning from kids. Every day we get to see the future of the world forming in front of us. And we get to learn more about ourselves as we make difficult decisions every day.

We wrote this book to help you rise to the challenges so you can enjoy the benefits.

Your Guiding Principles

One of the challenges that all principals face is that we perform in front of an audience, so all our mistakes are public. Teachers, students, parents, and district personnel judge your performance without understanding the complexity of your job or the difficulties you face. You will be second-guessed, doubted, compared to unrealistic examples of best practice, criticized, and even mocked by many of the stakeholders you serve—and this is especially true for first-year principals. Every mistake you make—from a mispronounced name to a spelling error on a memo to toilet paper stuck on the bottom of your shoe when exiting a restroom—will be noticed and discussed.

How do you maintain your sanity, confidence, and reputation in this kind of fishbowl? You have to be a leader.

That may sound pat or overly simple. You're the principal—the boss—of *course* you have to be a leader, right? But *leadership* has hundreds of definitions. It's a concept that is complex, is personal, and means different things to different people.

When we talk about leadership, we're talking about one overarching concept: having guiding principles that govern the decisions we make. That means doing what is right, not what is easy. It means standing up for what's right, even if you're standing alone. Your guiding principles cannot be compromised even if doing so is politically expedient, pleases your superiors or subordinates, or leads to easier immediate consequences. This is not to say that a good leader operates with a "my way or the highway" mentality. It just means you measure all decisions against those guiding principles.

The most important guiding principle is that all decisions should help, not hurt, kids. For example, maybe you want to paint the school bathrooms with school colors, but the district will only buy white paint. Fighting the district over this is a poor use of energy, because white paint does not hurt kids. Effective leaders choose their battles wisely. They choose not on the basis of which battles they can win but rather on which battles they must fight to avoid violating their guiding principles.

Of course, standing up for your principles isn't always easy. If you become known for standing up for your principles, voicing opposition or support for issues based on those principles, then you may become a target. If you are unlikely to be manipulated or coerced, you can become a barrier for others, such as parents who want uncalled for special treatment for their children, teachers who want a policy changed for self-serving reasons, outside vendors who want access to your students for the purpose of marketing to them, and more. Not everyone has the best interests of students in mind. Some people want to make money. Others want to have influence. The possibility of being targeted as a leader for engaging in leader-like behaviors is one of the ironies of the leadership journey. At times you will feel anxious or like you are in a "lose-lose" situation. You may question whether your guiding principles are even correct.

The answer to these uncomfortable situations is to stay the course. In the words of Dr. Martin Luther King Jr., "The time is always right to do what is right." If you measure your next steps according to your guiding principles, you will find that staying the course—even when the course feels like an uphill slog—is the correct path.

Not all leaders win trophies or awards. Unfortunately, some leaders are sacrificed by their superiors for maintaining an unpopular decision in the face of opposition. Those people pay a painful price in terms of their careers, their reputations, and even their faith in their own leadership. Those who refuse to allow their pitfalls to define them discover a freedom unknown to the average person. Once one has endured a leadership fall from grace and comes through on the other side, one doesn't fear it anymore. Your guiding principles remain the same and the costs don't seem as expensive. When leaders are doing the right thing, they are valued only because the demand is so great and the supply of principled, committed leaders unafraid to do what is right can be small.

Others recognizing that you operate in this manner is not as important as you knowing it. Others judge leaders based on their own perceptions and often their own "baggage." Successful leaders spend little time trying to control others' inaccurate assessments. Instead, they lead with courage. They follow Dr. King's words, and although there will be some sleepless nights along the way, the journey is invigorating and worth the trouble.

One thing that makes the job so compelling is that the principal is a safety net. We are often a kid's last chance to be redeemed, to be saved, to be loved. The kids who need us the most are the square pegs who are tired of round holes. They haven't been turned around by a teacher, coach, or counselor. They are in trouble, and their behavior often screams a compelling reminder that the kids who need love the most often act like they deserve it the least. Principals save lives, sometimes just because they are there. Being a significant adult to a child can result in such satisfaction.

How to Use This Book

The *Principal's Survival Guide* is designed to help with a wide range of things principals have to do but may not have had formal training in, from setting up your master calendar to hiring teachers to communicating with parents—and on and on. If you are an experienced principal, we believe you will find a fresh perspective in this book and at least a handful of helpful new tips. If you are a first-year principal, congratulations on your promotion! As you begin your first year, you are jumping on a nonstop roller coaster, and you will want this book along for the ride. Whatever your experience level, the advice in this book is meant to help you manage the twists, turns, drops, and loop-the-loops that are part of being a principal. You *can* get organized, manage, and lead in a way that gives you both the time and the peace of mind to get the sleep you need, at least most nights.

The systems, policies, advice, tips, and strategies in this book have all been forged from the question at the heart of our primary guiding principle: Is this good for kids? We believe these ideas will help you withstand the scrutiny, make decisions with confidence, and enjoy what truly is one of the greatest jobs in the world. You'll learn meat-and-potatoes things like what to do during morning drop-off, how to furnish your office on the cheap, and how to handle a group of angry parents. You'll also learn how to handle broader issues such as absence policies, talking to the media, and helping teachers fulfill their potential. You'll get tips to help you stay organized, learn from your experiences, and take care of yourself amid the stress and whirling pressures. This book is not about educational policy, improving assessment scores, or career-building. Those important topics are well-covered in other books. Rather, this book is about the nuts and bolts of being the best leader you can be—every day.

The book is organized like a handbook: You can use the table of contents to guide your reading, skipping around to chapters that can help you at any given time. Of course, you'll get the most out of the book if you read it all.

Chapters 1 and 2 cover the first few weeks after you are hired, and they're all about setting yourself up so you feel confident and prepared for the coming year. What do you do first? What do you need to take care of before the first day of school? What should you focus on next? What is your vision for the school? **Chapter 3** leads you through the process of assessing which policies are working in your school and which ones need to be revised—and guides you through the revision process. **Chapters 4 through 6** help you assess your staff and understand how to support all teachers, no matter their experience or aptitude. **Chapter 7** is all about establishing your leadership style and leading your school through necessary changes. **Chapter 8** provides guidance for documenting decisions and events so you can learn from your mistakes and successes as well as justify decisions when needed. **Chapter 9** is about communication with the outside world. Finally, **Chapter 10** pulls the focus in tight on yourself with advice on how to stay rested, healthy, and happy through all the ups and downs.

Besides the ideas, tips, and guidelines in every chapter, you'll also find "Stories from the Field." These examples are composite stories gathered from our experiences and the experiences of hundreds of principals we've known, including those we've worked with personally and many more we've met at conferences and through networking all over the United States. We have changed details to protect the identities of the people in them.

This is a book written *for* principals *by* principals, and it's important to remember that *you* were chosen to be a principal because someone saw your leadership potential. All you can ask from yourself is the same thing you ask from your teachers and students: Try your best and always be growing. We hope that as you continue on your path this book will be helpful in that continued growth. This is important work, and what you do matters.

We would love to hear how this book has helped you in your career as a principal. If you have stories or questions for us, you can reach us through our publisher at help4kids@freespirit.com.

Susan Kessler
April Snodgrass
Andrew Davis

CHAPTER ONE

Getting Started

Maybe the promotion to principal was long overdue, or maybe you simply were in the right place at the right time. Either way, you've got the job now, and you have more to think about than your brain can process. Where do you start? Do you walk into a school and say, "I am the new sheriff in town," or do you quietly observe the status quo? Do you introduce yourself by your first name or use the formal salutation of Mr., Ms., or Dr.? What do you wear? How do you transition your predecessor out? What about setting up your office?

Here is what you do: breathe. In and out. Repeat often, and remind yourself, "Rome wasn't built in a day." Begin by making a to-do list, adding items regardless of how big or small they are. That way you won't have to keep remembering all the balls you're juggling at once.

Then you prioritize. This chapter hits some of the high spots of a new principal's to-do list.

Get "The Look"

First things first: You have to look like the principal. What does that mean to you, and how does that play into your leadership style? Does that mean ties with apples and school buses printed on them, or a suit every day? You may be promoted in the summer, which traditionally means business casual clothing for principals until school starts, but perhaps that is not right for you. It depends where on you are in your particular situation.

For example, if you're young—or look young—and this is your first principal job, dressing up is probably better. You do not want to give anyone reason to take you less-than-seriously, and let's be honest: Some people will quickly judge you by how you dress.

As a general rule, the principal should look more dressed up than others in the building. The principal's example also sets the level of professional dress in the building. For example, if you come to work wearing jeans, then others will think jeans are okay as well. You may have heard this expression that we often tell teachers: "It's a lot easier to lighten up than tighten up." The same can be said for the principal's personal image. Dressing down if your initial style was too formal is easier than dressing up if your style was too casual.

The decision about what you wear is yours, but keep in mind that what you wear makes a statement.

Make Your Workplace Work

You have to have an office to do your work. You need a desk, phone, and computer from day one. You'll also want to decorate it somehow. Some people like to display their diplomas and awards while others think that looks too self-promoting. That choice is up to you. Displaying school colors shows your loyalty to the school, and it's easy to order a few custom-colored pom-poms online. Artwork students have made and photographs of your own family are personal touches that send a clear message that you care about children.

You will definitely need (at least) one bulletin board to hang calendars, memos, schedules, etc., and it's invaluable to have a bulletin board specifically to display positive press. These bits of good news have much value, whether they come from the local *PennySaver* or a major metropolitan newspaper. A locking file cabinet that keeps employee records and other sensitive files private and safe is critical and can double as a place to store your purse or bag each day. You can also lock your personal keys in the file cabinet and only carry school keys around your neck or on a belt loop while at school to ensure your own belongings are safe.

What if your predecessor is still sitting in the principal's chair when you start the job? People will be watching to see what you do, and you won't win any popularity points if you oust the former principal from her office. If you are appointed on June 1 and the principal's last day is June 30, then unless the principal moves out on her own accord, your best bet is to find a satellite office to do your work within the school. Even if the principal was controversial or unpopular, she will have followers and admirers, and alienating those people is a huge mistake.

What if you've got an office but the furniture is mismatched and shabby? Schools seldom have money available for furniture, and if you do have money you likely will want to spend it on student desks and tables. But as principal of your school, your office represents you as a CEO of that organization, and you don't look "large and in charge" leaning over a milk crate that is holding your laptop as you type. We have two words for you: used furniture. Liquidators buy and sell used office furniture when organizations change hands or close down. You can outfit your office with furniture that technically is used—and would be way out of a school's price range when new—but that looks and works great. It's a perfect way to economically outfit your office to look like a leader's office.

Your office is your workplace, and your staff needs to know that you do not anticipate people going in there in your absence. It is wise to re-key your office and give a key only to trusted individuals because that is the only way to know who actually has access.

Get Access

Districts use a wide variety of computer programs to keep themselves organized and to do a variety of jobs, from hiring to taking attendance to analyzing student data. Some of those systems include the following.

- **Student data system:** student addresses, demographics, schedules, transcripts, and attendance
- **Personnel data system:** teacher demographics, pay levels, education, certifications, sick time availability, recommendations for hire, background checks and clearances, and retirements
- **Achievement data system:** data on standardized tests by student, by subject, by grade level, by teacher, and by school; predictions of student success on standardized tests
- **Accounting/purchasing system:** requesting purchase orders, processing requisitions, and approving checks; collecting and crediting monies
- **Maintenance system:** recording building needs, maintenance items, upgrades
- **Inventory system:** tracking books, technology, copy machines, and equipment checked out to employees

If you're new to the district, you will need to learn all of these systems and ensure that you get access in a timely manner. Even if you're not new to the district, you will probably need to spend time learning these systems. While you might have some experience with them, generally a principal will have different levels of access than an assistant principal because the jobs and responsibilities are different. Things that were grayed out for you when you were an assistant principal may now be usable, or you'll need to learn programs that you may have known about but didn't have access to. Your supervisor or a veteran principal at the same tier level could tell you how to get the access you need. It may be as simple as sending an email to the right person, or you may be required to attend training, but the sooner you start asking, the sooner you can get what you need.

You also need access to the school's bank accounts. From the first day you officially begin work as the principal, you are legally accountable for every penny that is spent. You will need to go to the bank to take the former principal off the account as the signer of checks and add yourself. You may not want to spend any money the first week until you evaluate how things work at your school, but you do not want anyone else spending money either. The buck stops with you, and you are in charge of all bucks.

Who Else Works Here?

It seems like a straightforward question. But in reality, it can sometimes be hard to pin down. How many teachers, administrators, secretaries, cafeteria workers, and custodians work here? Ask for a payroll printout that shows everyone's full- or part-time status. Ms. Falco and Mr. Bernardino may share one position, but if you do not know their FTE (full-time equivalent), you may think you have 42 teachers when you are only budgeted for 41. But you have 42 teachers (some with part-time allocations) who fill 41 positions.

Make a list of everyone's job title and FTE, and take a look at your vacancies. It is usually better for you to hire new teachers, rather than your predecessor. Some new principals might feel it's easier to let the outgoing principal handle this, but you know what you want in a staff member, and your predecessor may have wanted different attributes. You might not have a lot of time, but hiring staff members is actually the most important job a principal does. You can involve other team members or a leadership team, but you must have the head seat at the hiring table. See section entitled "High-Quality New Teachers: What to Look For" for more about hiring teachers.

The School's Mini-Makeover

With the rare exception of brand new buildings, most schools have some cosmetic defects or improvements that can be made, and if you start during the summer, you have time to take care of these things. A newly painted area or some freshly planted flowering bushes can make a big difference. Bright, kid-friendly colors and positive messages are environmental magnets for kids, teachers, and parents. They make a difference because they impact everyone's attitude about the school environment. When teachers and students return from break and see that the school *looks* good, they're likely to feel that things will *be* good.

These cosmetic improvements help instill school pride, and they show your attention to detail.

Meeting with Staff and Families

Secretaries are used to adapting to what their supervisor wants, but they can't adapt to what they do not know. Meet with your office support staff early on to set clear expectations about a wide variety of things including:
- How the phone is to be answered
- How questions and concerns are routed to the principal or others
- How foot traffic is handled

- How upset parents are handled
- How salespeople are handled
- What to do when students want to see the principal or teachers
- The keeping of your calendar and scheduling of your meetings
- Who relieves the secretary for lunch

Meeting with secretaries is important because they are your gatekeepers. The way they communicate—both formally and informally—represents you, so be clear about how you want communication handled. Think of the damage a secretary can do by saying, "I am sorry but Principal Hall does not meet with parents without an appointment" as opposed to "Have you spoken with the teacher? Principal Hall will want you to do that before he schedules your meeting." In a large school where there are several assistant principals, secretaries need to point the parent to the assistant principal assigned to the student as a matter of procedure, but there are times when parents want to see the principal in charge. Principals need to meet with parents when they demand a meeting, and the secretaries need to know that you will do so.

It's also hugely beneficial to meet with teachers and parents when you can. For these stakeholders, there is no substitute for looking you in the eye and hearing what you have to say. Some teachers and parents will be hungry for this opportunity, so if they reach out to you, embrace it. (See section entitled "Communicating with Students and Parents" for more on meeting with parents.) Your relationships with parents and teachers are integral to moving the school forward.

Different people will want different things from you. Some may request a sit-down meeting while others would like a hand shake at an informal gathering. Neither is necessarily superior—make yourself available for both.

Meeting with Administrators

Most principals beginning a new appointment will be joining a staff that has at least one assistant principal as part of the administrative structure, and you may have as many as seven assistant principals reporting to you. How do you maintain consistency among many administrators? How do you keep parents, students, and teachers from employing the manipulative "mom says no so ask dad and hope for a different answer" tactic? And how do you foster *teamwork* among the administrative team?

One word answers all those questions: *communication*. How you want things handled in your school needs to be explicitly communicated among all administrators. For example, an effective strategy in a large school where several people are disciplining students is to have an internal discipline matrix that lists offenses and the consequences that go with them. (We do not advocate publishing this document, because there will be exceptions, and some students and behaviors will warrant more or less severe consequences depending on the situation.) It is a good idea to meet with your administrators to go through the painstaking process of establishing what are the most important behaviors to reduce at your school and how to do it.

As head principal, you need to be decisive and clear, not only to make sure your school runs efficiently, but also because the assistant principalship is a means of preparing for the important role of head principal. Assistant principals may not agree with how you do something and tell themselves, "When I'm the principal, I'll do it differently." That is the entire point! Assistant principals may agree or disagree with a strategy or philosophy of yours, but they can only make informed opinions about these things if they are *informed*. Communicating your beliefs and guiding principles enables assistants to continually compare their own philosophical positions to yours. This process allows future leaders to give thought to the important decisions the principal has to make before they have to make them. That leadership development is the most helpful thing a mentor can do for protégés.

Some principals meet weekly with their assistants at a regular time. Some meet only as necessary. The important thing is to get everyone

on the same page. Things that regularly need to be discussed:
- Days and times you will be out of the building, and who is appointed principal designee for those times
- Days and times assistant principals will be out of the building
- Unusual schedule changes or special events
- Upcoming planning: when are the report card deadlines and parent conference days be scheduled?
- Review of data: how are students progressing and what are we doing to help those who are struggling?
- Review of teacher performance: are teachers having classroom management issues, high absenteeism, or a negative attitude, or who is going above and beyond and needs to be recognized?

Revisit these topics weekly because the information can change so frequently. A school with several assistant principals may have more than one hundred teachers. You will need to rely on your assistants to help keep you informed since you can't be everywhere at all times.

Information sharing with assistant principals can be done via email; however, leading assistant principals is incredibly important and is most effective in face-to-face interactions. The administrative team is critical to an effectively run school, and if everyone is too busy to talk to one another, what could result is five small schools all running within the same building rather than five sub-parts of one well-coordinated machine.

Schedules and Calendars

As principal, you'll have many demands on your time, and you'll need a way to keep ahead of what is going on. Having a master calendar for the school, a detailed calendar for yourself, as well as plans for daily routines will help keep your head above water during the school year.

Master the Schedule

If you're hired in the summer, the master schedule—the schedule that shows when, where, and by whom all classes are taught—has probably already been developed. Unless there are a lot of problems with the master schedule, go with it for now. Revamping it when you're not yet familiar with the talents of your staff could result in a schedule that is good for teachers but not necessarily a schedule that is good for the students.

What kind of problems should you look for? If the schedule is grounded in adult wants rather than student needs, then you will need to make changes. At the high school level, look at the course requests and see if the master schedule matches. For example, if you have 200 students who need English IV, you need at least six sections of English IV in your schedule. You also want the right teachers teaching the courses. You want your top-level teachers in your most important classes (those that count for your state testing and those that prepare students for life after high school). At all levels, make sure teacher certifications match up with the classes they teach. You don't want a teacher certified in biology teaching Spanish just because she happens to also speak Spanish. Also pay attention to the needs of students, and make sure those who need smaller classes or particular classes, such as English language learners or special education students, get them.

If the schedule isn't done when you arrive—or if the existing schedule is too problematic to fix—then you need to get working, because the schedule is a prerequisite to identifying personnel needs. Even though you are the principal, you do not have to do the schedule alone. If you are inexperienced at scheduling, ask your supervisor to recommend another principal who can help you. And you'll be able to see how another school has organized its school day for success.

Master Calendar

No matter the level of your school, you'll have a wide variety of school events, and a school master calendar is essential for you and your staff to keep track of them all. If one does not already exist at the school, you'll want to create a master calendar as soon as possible. Include information from the school district about school holidays, conference days, progress report and report card days, and assessment dates. Add school-specific events such as PTO/PTA meetings, field days, musicals, sporting events, open houses, school fund-raisers, and club events. Add field trips, assemblies, faculty meetings, and faculty-wide professional development to this calendar as they are determined.

When placing items on the calendar, don't just name the event, but include time, location, and any requirements such as AV equipment, seating, people needed to supervise, or whether you must attend. Having all this information in a central location helps prevent conflicting events and ensures that everyone is in the know so they can plan accordingly. Many schools use an electronic calendar that all staff can access and add to via their own computers and devices, while others have one person who maintains the master calendar and handles submissions to be added. You do not necessarily have to be the one to coordinate the calendar, but we recommend that you approve the adding of events.

Principal's Calendar

Your own calendar is separate from the master calendar but needs to include all of the information from the master calendar, plus appointments, meetings, and trainings that you're required to attend. Add your personal appointments to the calendar, too. Principals need to get their teeth cleaned every six months like everyone else, and maintaining a single calendar for professional and personal appointments will reduce confusion.

You may want to share this calendar with your secretary if your secretary makes appointments for you, but otherwise this is a personal calendar for you to keep track of what you need to do.

Daily Routine

When starting a new job, you'll want to establish a daily routine immediately. This consistency will help you as well as your staff and students. While there will always be unforeseen events that come up and force you to make changes to your schedule, establishing a daily schedule and routine will prevent you from wasting time and help you make progress toward meeting the school's goals and your vision a reality.

Here are a few guidelines to consider.

Drop-Off Time

Morning drop-off is a great time to see and be seen and interact with kids, parents, and teachers in the hustle and bustle of the school day. Whether it is working the drop-off line for car riders, being present when students get off buses, greeting students in the lobby, or rotating through the cafeteria during breakfast, taking the time to be visible sends a clear signal that you are involved and getting to know your students and their families is important to you.

The downside of being visible is that it can often feel as if you are on a raging river being pelted from all sides by parents, staff, and students constantly bringing situations to your attention. People will approach you to discuss a wide variety of situations. These interactions are often short, and it is important for you to be present and to make that time count. If people feel like they've been heard, it solidifies your leadership. Conversely, if a stakeholder feels slighted, snubbed, or ignored, these relationships will soon manifest themselves into bigger problems down the road.

It is also important to keep track of what you say, agree to, or approve during these interactions. We recommend having some way to keep notes about these interactions as well as other decisions that you make during the day. You might carry around a clipboard with a notepad or a small notepad in your pocket, or you might use your phone to record information. Do what works best for you, but regardless of your system, the few seconds it takes to record these interactions can save you hours down the road. See section entitled "Document Your Interactions" for more information.

Morning Announcements

By handling the morning announcements, you are setting the tone for the entire school day. Decide what tone you want to set and how you will go about it. Will you recite the Pledge of Allegiance, observe a moment of silence, play a song, or invite student participation? Will you close with a tagline such as "No one knows what you can achieve until you try"?

Announcements take up very little of the school day, but they can impact the overall school culture. By handling the morning announcements, you let students and staff know that you are in charge, which is comforting to them. If you'll be away from the building and unable to give the morning announcements, have a procedure in place for a designee to handle them so the school knows that even if you are out or unavailable, leadership is still present.

Classroom Visits

Schedule time so you can rotate through classes during the day and monitor student learning. This action helps you keep a pulse on the school atmosphere for the day. It also helps hold teachers accountable and sends the message to teachers and students that instructional time is valued and monitored. You can also make note of positive behaviors and particularly good lessons or other moments to talk about with teachers and students later. Following up with a teacher in a brief note or hallway conversation about something positive you noticed during your rounds will help boost morale and let staff know that you are paying attention. The same is true for students.

Regularly Scheduled Meetings

Set up regular meetings with assistant principals, instructional coaches, counselors, and other people in the building. Many principals schedule these meetings on specific days of the week at specific times, such as 3:33 on Mondays, so people will remember these are standing appointments. Encourage staff (and yourself!) to put these meetings on their electronic calendars so they can set up an alert to remind them.

Many times, administrators participate in special education meetings for IEPs and support teams. If your attendance is required at these meetings, establish that they are always scheduled during certain days and times of the week otherwise you will find your schedule overtaken by them. With this system in place, you also help the many different case managers and counselors know when to schedule them.

One-on-One Meetings

In addition to staff meetings, administrator meetings, and other regularly occurring meetings, you will want to schedule occasional one-on-one meetings with faculty, staff, and members of the wider community throughout the school year. You might want to set up office hours where faculty and staff can sign up for a time to meet. Or you might prefer to have an open-door policy where people can pop in at their leisure when they need to discuss something. You may also want to schedule standing meetings with certain staff such as your secretary.

When setting up meetings with people outside of the school building, some principals prefer to set up all of their own appointments while others may give their schedule to their secretary and allow him to schedule the appointments. These are personal decisions based on what you are comfortable with and what works best for you. You might decide to change if your first method does not work. If you start with an open-door policy but can't get work done because of people randomly popping in to chat with you, then you may want to shift to office hours where your door is "open" at certain times and "closed" (literally or metaphorically) at others.

Principal Time with Students

As principal, you may find that you spend very little time working individually with students. Due to all of the demands on your time, especially from those outside of the building, individual face time with students can be nonexistent if you're not careful. It's important to be out of your office during arrival, dismissal, class transitions, and lunch in order to build relationships with students. Being seen by students, knowing their names, and mentioning something specific about them can go a long way in building student engagement within the school. When you can cite a specific positive characteristic of a student, it makes that student feel special. This is another reason that being present in classrooms is so important. What you observe in a classroom can then become a conversation starter with a student.

This does not mean that you won't ever meet individually with students. Especially at the high school and middle school levels, students will often request to meet with you. They may want to discuss a problem with a teacher or an assistant principal or share an idea for a new club or school event. You will want to decide how to handle these requests. How will students request these meetings? By email? By text message? Through your secretary? When will you meet with them? During lunch? During class time? When do you direct them to someone else instead of them meeting with you? These decisions are up to you as the principal.

Observations and Conferences

As the school year progresses, build time into your daily schedule for teacher observations and teacher conferences. These evaluations can become time-devourers if you don't plan accordingly. Many successful principals make a spreadsheet with teachers' names in the first column and subsequent columns observations required based on a teacher's certification and prior year's evaluations. (This is determined by the state or district where the school is located.) You can break the evaluations into cycles. Being able to announce when observations will take place helps alleviate teacher anxiety.

In addition, if the evaluation cycle requires unannounced observations, many principals will give teachers a window of when these evaluations will take place. By using a spreadsheet, you can quickly and easily keep track of teacher evaluations, one of your primary roles as instructional leader. Scheduling all observations on your calendar ahead of time, including those that are unannounced, can help you ensure that all observations are completed in a timely manner.

***

With all these seemingly pesky details, the idea is to lay your groundwork early—setting the tone, planning your schedule, and figuring out the specifics—so once the school year gets going and gets hectic, you won't have to worry as much about keeping your wits together for the daily routines. You'll have more mental capacity to devote to the bigger things.

CHAPTER TWO

Establishing a Vision and Goals

Whether it's your first job as a principal or your first year in a new school, you will have a lot to do in the beginning. As you're getting a feel for the school culture and establishing yourself as a leader, you might find yourself treading on some very thin ice in those early days. Knowing where to look for the "cracks" can help you avoid crashing into ice-cold waters. By soliciting input from stakeholders[1] and expressing a clear vision for your school, you're more likely to win them over. Once you've established that vision, you and your leadership team can start developing the goals that will enable the school to reach that vision.

Vision and Goals Defined

Having a **vision** for your school means beginning with the end in mind. A vision describes what the ultimate "win" will be for a

---

[1] Stakeholders are the people you serve and work with as principal—the teachers, students, parents, community members, and staff.

school. It should have student learning at its core and speak to what the school will look like when everything falls into place.

A vision is a reach, but it still needs to be attainable. Imagine a person who weighs 300 pounds with a vision of losing 100 pounds. This is not easy, but it's attainable through work. Losing 200 pounds and becoming a fashion model might be too much of a reach. For a school, getting 100 percent of the students on grade level for reading is an example of an attainable reach. Getting 100 percent of the students to receive a perfect score on the ACT or the SAT is not.

A leader cannot develop the vision alone. It's your job to lead the process of reviewing the data for student achievement, attendance, teacher professional development, and school climate studies, and to use all of that information to establish the state of the school. You will do this with a group comprised of faculty, staff, parents, and other interested parties.

Your team will also need to set goals. A **goal** is an action step toward achieving the vision—think of each goal as a building block along the way. Our overweight individual might have a goal of losing 20 pounds within 4 months to move toward the vision of being 100 pounds lighter over the course of 20 months. If only 25 percent of students in your school are reading on grade level, and the vision is for 100 percent, then the first goal might be to increase that to

30 percent by a certain date. After that, set a goal for 50 percent, and so on.

Determine Your School's Priorities

In order to create a vision and set goals, you must first get a clear picture of where the school stands. What kind of circumstances are you inheriting? Was the previous principal a beloved leader who retired after many years in the job, or was he removed after only one or two years of service? Has the school been making progress, or has it failed to move in the right direction? Is the school viewed as a "good" school that has hit a few bumps or a "bad" school that people are afraid to send their kids to?

You may get appointed at the end of the previous school year and have the entire summer to gather information, or you may get the job days before the school year starts—or, worse yet, once the school year has already started. Even if time is tight, it's critical that you find a way to gather some basic pieces of information, including information about your stakeholders; data about the school's performance and climate; and clarity about the expectations of your supervisors.

Get Feedback from Stakeholders

The true resource of any school is ultimately the personnel who work there. In order to understand your school's priorities, you need to meet as many of these people as soon as possible to begin to develop a working relationship.

In some circumstances, the transition allows for you to sit down and discuss personnel and other school items with the prior principal. This meeting with your predecessor is an invaluable opportunity to gain an understanding of the nuts and bolts of the school, but remember that this information is coming from one person's perspective. Be careful not to become biased or make judgments based on this information alone. If meeting with your predecessor is not possible, review personnel files and evaluations to begin to gather information.

If you are hired during the summer, get discussions going right away by hosting separate meetings with the staff and parents before school starts so you can share your background and learn more about the school from their perspective. You will also learn much about the teachers from their views on the school and the students. Do they speak of the school in a positive way? Do they think all students are capable of being successful? Do they get along with their peers? Parents' comments about teachers can also provide insight. These comments can help determine teachers' strengths and weaknesses which can help in your planning.

If you are hired close to—or after—the start of school, then schedule meetings with faculty and parents within your first two weeks. While you may have already needed to set your vision and goals without getting all of the input you might like, it is still important to meet with them and get a feel for their views of the school.

Besides these formal meetings, look for opportunities in the summer and the early weeks of school to chat informally with teachers, staff, parents, students, and other members of the school community. Take time to engage in conversations with teachers when they come in to work on their room or with parents when they come to register their kids for school. A positive personal interaction can go a long way toward establishing you in your school as well as providing information you'll need to guide your vision and goal setting.

Conversations with teachers and parents can help develop your vision and goals by bringing to light reoccurring themes or areas to address. If an issue keeps coming up in conversations with different people, then you know you likely need to address it. You can also learn what stakeholders value, which is important information when crafting the vision.

Stories from the Field

Parents and staff were concerned about the principal who had been in place for a few years. They expressed their concern to the central office. School achievement scores had declined, but more concerning was the culture of the school. Many parents, teachers, and students felt that their voices were no longer being heard. Teachers were fearful of speaking out. During the summer, the district transferred the principal and promoted an assistant principal from another school with ties to the community.

Right away, the new principal held meetings with teachers and parents. Acknowledging these stakeholders' concerns about the previous principal, she told them that she intended to share information freely and that she intended to seek input from them. She made it clear, though, that while she intended to listen, she would make decisions based on what the school needed. She provided data that showed where declines had occurred in achievement and where significant gaps existed between groups of students. All information would be reviewed, she said, but her highest

> **priority would be raising student achievement.**

This scenario highlights the importance of gathering information about your new school as soon as you can. You won't be able to establish goals and a vision until you do. Note that the new principal solicited feedback from stakeholders but clearly asserted that she was the final decision maker.

Review School Data

Schools have hard data such as climate surveys, test scores, poverty rates, mobility rates, and teacher turnover rates. Schools also have soft data such as comments made by students, teachers, and parents; feelings that those stakeholders had toward the previous administration; and the way the school is viewed in the community. You will need to look at as many different types of data as possible to get a clear view of the problems and ascertain which problems need to be fixed first. Regardless of the overall state of the school, certain issues will always be more pressing than others.

Data from previous climate surveys will serve you well in establishing goals to implement your vision and in checking the community's interest in the vision. If your vision relates to student achievement, but parent and staff surveys show that those stakeholders think it's more important that school be "fun," then implementing goals regarding student achievement will be a laborious task. It will take many meetings and research-proven strategies showing learning can be fun *and* student achievement can increase.

Review the school's state testing data to see the achievement and growth results of the school. It is also important to determine any trends in the data over the past few years. Some things to look for:

- **The trends of specific math and/or reading scores.** Are they increasing, declining, or flattening over the past few years?
- **Performance of different subgroups.** Who is being helped by current practice, and who is being left behind?
- **Specific teachers' class results.** Which teachers are being the most or least effective?

Once you have found the trends, patterns, and outliers, you can work to figure out the reasons behind the data. Did Ms. Flannery get better scores because she used different strategies, or was it because she had the top performing students? Did students with disabilities do worse because of the effectiveness of an individual teacher or because all teachers had low expectations? Figuring out the reasons behind the data takes a bit of detective work but will lead to increased performance of students if results are used to help in your planning process.

Reviewing prior year teacher evaluations will help you focus your staff's professional development needs.

In addition to older data, send out a survey to families and staff to gather new data. Web-based survey tools make gathering and analyzing input quick and easy. Here are some questions to consider for surveys of both teachers and parents:

- What are the current strengths of the school?
- What are current needs of the school?
- What does the school do well?
- What can the school improve on immediately?
- What do you think is the purpose of school?
- What would you change about the school?
- In what areas does the staff need professional development?
- What are the students really good at?
- What do students need to focus more on?

Set a firm deadline for responding to the survey, and once it passes, immediately analyze the results. What trends do you notice? Some of the data may reinforce obvious areas of concern and strengths that you already knew about. Some information might be surprising or shed light on strengths and weaknesses you weren't aware of. Pull out the highlights of your analysis and communicate them to families and staff in a timely way. Otherwise, when surveys are given again, people won't bother to complete them. They will think that their response to the previous survey went straight to the bottom of one of those gargantuan piles of papers on your desk.

Understand the Expectations of Your Supervisors

The reality of any job is that if your boss is not happy with what you're doing, you may not be doing it for long. If expectations of performance were not shared with you during the hiring process, then make sure to schedule a meeting with your supervisor to find out what success looks like from his point of view.

Have your data ready before this meeting and be able to intelligently discuss it so your supervisor sees that you have a clear understanding of what you're inheriting—and also, simply, so *he* knows what you're inheriting. Your boss will already have a view of the school that may or may not be based on real data, so sharing that data may keep your supervisor from setting unrealistic goals for you.

Create the Vision and Goals

After you have gathered feedback from your stakeholders, reviewed the school data, and understood the expectations of your supervisors, you are ready to establish the vision and create goals. The development of the vision is crucial for the new leader, and ultimately that vision must have student learning and achievement at its core. Once the vision is in place, you will use it as a touchstone upon which all decisions are vetted. If you try to make decisions to placate one or more groups without keeping true to the school's vision, you will soon find yourself lost in a forest—and find that the school is not progressing.

When developing a vision statement, the process is as important as the product. Convene a school leadership team made up of grade-level leaders, team leaders, department chairs, assistant principals, and yourself, and start by developing consensus about what the school will ultimately look like. This will likely take several hours. The next step is to describe the environment that would support such a school. Putting these two ingredients together, you can craft your vision statement. Your vision statement might look something like this:

- Central School is committed to providing students with exemplary instruction designed to educate the whole child so that all children can become productive members of the community.
- The faculty, staff, and students of Central School will provide a nurturing environment where personal growth and responsibility are

valued and academic excellence is a daily pursuit.
- It is the vision of Central School to work in partnership with families and the community to create and maintain a safe, positive, diverse, and challenging learning environment.

Next, your team will set the goals. Your goals need to be specific, measurable, attainable/achievable, relevant/realistic, and time-related/time-bound. Such goals are often known as SMART goals, and each of them should contribute directly to achieving your vision. Examples of goals include:
- Students will grow one grade level in reading by the end of the school year.
- Seventy percent of third graders will attain a score of "proficient" on the spring math exam.

It is important that the goals represent clear, positive steps toward your vision and be realistic. If 30 percent of third graders were proficient in math last year, a jump to 70 percent is unrealistic. Achievement gains greater than 10 percent are not impossible to achieve, but they are typically less realistic than more modest goals.

Though you will have already met with stakeholders to establish your vision for the school, you may want to seek additional input from them during this goal-setting time. This is a great way to show staff and parents that you value their input and that they will help shape those goals. You can do this by holding "open house" meetings where you discuss your vision and ask, "What is going well?" and "What do we need to improve on?"

However, it's not your questions or stakeholders' answers that matter most. It's your response to their answers. When people give honest feedback and criticism to their principal, they are taking a huge risk, and they are watching to see how you respond. It's not enough just to gather feedback from stakeholders. You have to use the feedback and communicate how you used it.

Not only is the information you gather through discussions and surveys valuable, but seeking this information will also help you get buy-in from your stakeholders. When you can stand in front of the faculty or a parent group and discuss your goals for the school—goals that were shaped by their input and that will help change the culture and climate for the school—they will be more motivated to embrace these changes. You will already be gaining traction with stakeholders, gathering followers, and building a consensus.

This does not mean that all stakeholders will be on board. Getting all parties to embrace your vision and goals is the next step in your process.

Keep Long-Term Gains in Sight

Once you have established your vision and goals, publish the vision on your school's website and post it throughout the building and in every classroom. You may want to also add the vision statement—or a tagline that can be pulled from it, such as "where personal growth is valued and academic excellence is a daily pursuit"—on your email signature, school stationery, or any other place where it can be seen often by your school and community. Recite the vision during morning announcements to help continually remind everyone what they are working toward. This is an important part of building support for the vision and goals.

If you're coming into a situation where you have to improve school culture, you may have to make difficult short-term decisions in order to reach your goals. Making decisions that are popular but hinder student achievement will doom you in the long run. For example, veteran teachers often do not want to teach high-stakes classes that have state assessment testing at the end of the year that will directly impact their evaluations. These classes often create tremendous pressure for the teacher because student performance is under the microscope during the entire year, up to and through the assessment. It might be popular among your staff to allow veteran teachers to teach low-stakes classes and have new teachers handling high-stakes classes, but if your veteran teachers are highly effective, then letting them teach low-stakes classes may not be the best decision for student achievement. Even decisions that may boost student achievement scores in the short term can sometimes make reaching long-term student growth more difficult. Teaching only items that are on the current grade-level test without giving any thought to future tests may set up students for failure later on. You have worked hard to reach this new position, and staying here will require making far-sighted decisions, even if they are unpopular.

One area where it's all too easy to make popular short-term decisions that can be damaging in the future is faculty changes.

Stories from the Field

A new principal changed the schedule of a teacher who had become an institution at the school. This teacher had not only been at the school through several administrators, but she also held a leadership role. Since she was an established teacher who was well-respected by other faculty members and parents, her views would easily gather support. But she always seemed to take a contrarian approach to school and district initiatives. In addition,

students with disabilities and students living in poverty failed to demonstrate academic growth in classes she taught.

Parents and students demanded the teacher be reinstated to her original schedule, but the district backed the principal, who withstood some intense criticism for this decision. Within two years, the program the teacher had led had grown even more in her absence, and student achievement and growth had improved for all students.

You may have to make a change that negatively impacts a well-loved but ineffective teacher. The short-term storm you'll have to weather—in the form of negative backlash from families and other teachers—is less important than what is best for the long-term success of the school.

Stories from the Field

A high school had had low attendance rates, high incidents of tardiness, low achievement scores, and an unsafe learning environment. Student attendance at school sporting events was low, and the school had not had a pep rally in years due to the threat of student fights.

The new principal announced that the school would have a pep rally the day of the first home football game. Parents, staff, and students said it wouldn't work. The new principal made it clear in advance that for students to attend the pep rally, they could not have any discipline referrals or be marked tardy during the pep rally week; students who failed to meet these guidelines would instead sit in silence in a study hall environment during the pep rally time.

The previous principal had made threats but often did not follow through on them, so students assumed it would be business as usual. However, just before the pep rally, those who had been tardy or received discipline referrals were pulled out of class and escorted to the auditorium, where they were seated with spaces between them and given their work. Teachers and administrators enforced the no talking rule.

Other faculty followed a detailed plan for managing the pep rally. Classes were called to the gym in an orderly fashion to prevent a mad rush of students coming to the gym at once. Teachers had assigned posts in the stands, helping prevent student disruptions during the pep rally. For most of those students, it was their first school pep rally. They didn't know when to cheer. The teachers and cheerleaders modeled how to have a fun but controlled pep rally.

At that same school, students had often been told to sit down during sporting events. The new administration created a student cheering section and enlisted some seniors to start painting themselves before the game and doing push-ups when their team scored. Those few actions quickly began turning the school spirit around. Students learned that when they followed the rules, they were entitled to have freedoms they had not had before at the school. Soon, one would hear students encouraging other students to be on time to class instead of loitering in the halls when the warning bell rang.

The short-term decisions this principal made seemed counterintuitive at first, but they began to lead to positive changes in the school. You have to be able to see the bigger picture and the potential of what the school can be—not just what the school currently is.

***

Regardless of the culture or history of the school you are joining, working with key stakeholders to create a vision and goals is one of the best ways to establish yourself as a leader; make connections with staff, students, and families; and begin to put your positive stamp on the school.

CHAPTER THREE

Policies, Practices, and Procedures

Policies, practices, and procedures—known as the 3Ps—make up the skeleton that holds up your school. They support everything that happens, and they guide every decision you make. Strong 3Ps establish an orderly environment where everyone knows the rules and expectations, and they help make your job easier.

A **policy** is a rule that governs how members of the school conduct their business. Policies can be sent down from the federal, state, or local government or be developed by the school board or principal. A **practice** is how the business of the school is conducted. Practice is how policies are actually implemented, and without solid practice implementation, policies will often fail. **Procedures** are the steps that result in routines, habits, and expectations that define our practice. Procedures are often imbedded in policies or developed later to help with the implementation of policies and to help improve practice.

The 3Ps: Where to Start?

Every school needs 3Ps that are clear, thorough, and aligned with district policies in the following areas:

- **Grades.** Grades are the number one way that a school communicates student progress to the parents and guardians of students, and so it is highly important that clear grading policies be shared not only with staff, but also with parents and students.
- **Finances.** Finances can play a very large part in the running of a school, so it is necessary to have clear policies, practices, and procedures in place to ensure that this often under-taught but highly necessary area is covered.
- **Employee Relations.** It's a wasted day of learning for students when the teacher is out and no lesson plans are waiting, or worse, when a teacher is out frequently for no apparent reason. Employee absence is just one of many areas of employee relations that require clear policies.
- **Emergencies and Other Contingencies.** Depending on your location, you may have to practice fire, tornado, hurricane, earthquake, or any other natural disaster drills. You might be required to turn in

paperwork to your district or state proving that you practiced them. While the general procedures are the same, each building may have its own particular procedures depending on the number of outside doors and windows, or the layout of the school. Lockdown drills are also now a regular part of every school's emergency practice, so make sure those procedures are clear, work for your school, and are communicated to everyone involved, including substitute teachers in the building.

- **Running the School.** These are the day-to-day processes of running a school, from simple things like handling attendance to more complex things like bullying policies. From the moment the first bus rolls up and the first student walks through the door to the moment the last student goes home and the final practice is over, you need clear policies in place to ensure that all begins and ends well.

When you come into a new school, the first step is to understand and evaluate the existing 3Ps as quickly as possible. This can be done through surveying faculty and staff and interviewing the former principal if possible, as well as talking with key people such as assistant administrators, the bookkeeper, secretaries, department heads or content leaders, and so on. Getting the opinions of those who are affected by the school's 3Ps but who are not generally involved in their implementation can also help you. This group can include students, parents, and any community members who are actively involved in the school as well as those people who hired and will supervise you.

Once you understand the current 3Ps, assess what seems to be working and what needs to be improved. Put each of the 3Ps into one of three categories: needs to be changed immediately, can stay for now but will eventually need to be changed, and can stay as it is. To determine how to categorize each policy, practice, or procedure, ask the following questions:

How to Decide if a Policy, Practice, or Procedure Needs to Be Changed Immediately

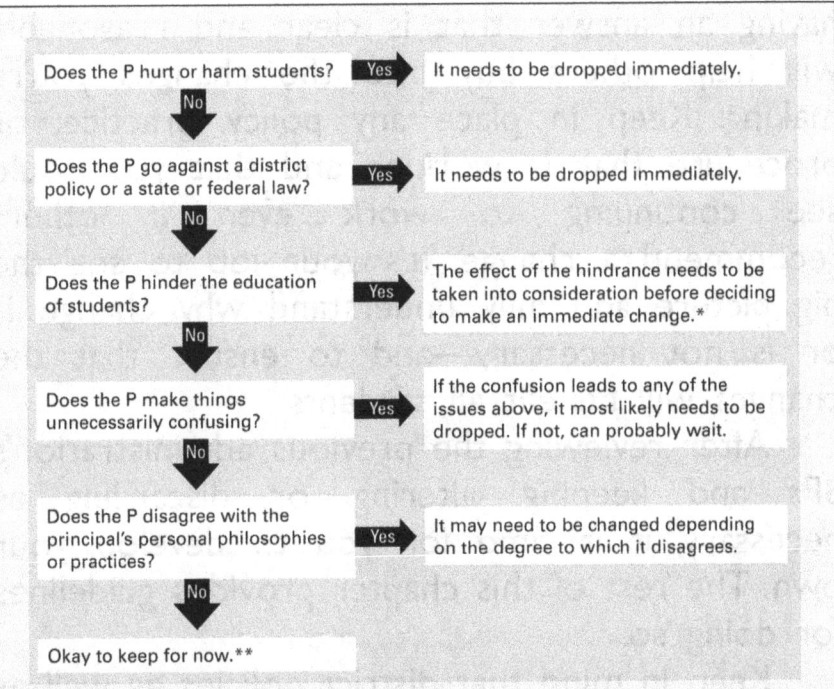

*A policy that states students don't have to practice writing after the state writing test is over is different from a policy that says students are not ever required to read on their own. You need to judge the seriousness of the situation and make changes accordingly.

**If the policy still does not seem right to you, figure out why. Depending on the answer, make your final decision. It is important to remember when making a change that if you cannot explain why you made the change, you are unlikely to get full support for it.

Changing policies, practices, or procedures without a reason won't benefit you or the school in any way. People will always ask why, and having an answer that is clear and reasonable will help others buy into the changes you're making. Keep in place any policy, practice, or procedure that is working and that you could see continuing to work even if others recommend a change. It's your job to see the big picture and fully understand why change is or is not necessary—and to ensure that the changes will benefit all students.

After reviewing the previous administration's 3Ps and keeping, altering, or discarding as necessary, it is time for you to develop your own. The rest of this chapter provides guidelines for doing so.

Keep in mind that district policies as well as state and federal laws must be used as a map for creating school-based policies. Never create a policy that goes directly against a district policy or a state or federal law, because if it is ever challenged, the district will not support what you have done. If there are potential questions about a policy, have it vetted by a trusted mentor. If you expect resistance from employees, approval from a district level supervisor is always a good idea to ensure district support.

3Ps for Grading

Many districts have grading policies, but they tend to be general since they apply to a wide variety of schools with students from grades preK to 12. It is important for a principal to really think about the grading policy and decide if it is specific enough to be measureable and clearly communicated to all involved. Following are some questions to consider when creating grading policies:

- **How many grades should a student earn during a grading period?** Should it be a required number or should it be up to teacher discretion? Having a required number makes monitoring easier, but finding the right number can be difficult. If you require too many, you may end up with teachers creating assignments just to meet the requirement. If too few, students who do poorly on one assignment can ruin their grade for the grading period. You may need to consider your answer to the next question first.
- **What should grades represent?** Grades might be an assessment of actual learning that students have done. They might also be based on homework completed; performance on final assessments only; timely completion of assignments; how neat and organized students' work is; students' ability to work well in the classroom environment; and their general conduct in and out of the classroom. This is a major discussion that needs to be held first within an administrative or leadership team

and then with the whole school faculty before any major changes are made.

- **Are there guidelines for how much a single assignment can be worth?** You might have a requirement that tests cannot be worth more than 40 percent of a student's total grade. This discussion is related to the question of how many grades will be earned per grading period.
- **What is an "acceptable" failure rate among students?** While in a perfect world, 100 percent of students are learning and succeeding, we do not live in a perfect world. Failure among students is a reality. But what rate of failure is too high? In a class of 30, if one or two students are failing, then it is likely due to the students' performance. But if 10 are failing, then there may be an issue with the teacher. Establish a failure rate for all classes that triggers an intervention if reached. Instill different levels of intervention based on the level of failure. For example, if a teacher has more than 10 percent failures, then the supervising administrator has a conversation with the teacher to ensure that interventions are being done. But if a teacher has more than 20 percent failures, then the teacher has to create a plan for intervention with failing students. You or a designated

administrator will review and monitor the plan.
- **How will grades be submitted?** If your school has an electronic gradebook that administrators have access to, this is a simple question. But if your school does not, then you need a straightforward way for you and the rest of your administrative team to see grades on a regular basis. Even with an electronic gradebook, you may want to require that a certain number of grades be filed at certain times; otherwise you will have teachers who will enter all grades at the end of the grading period, which makes it more difficult for them—and parents and students—to track progress. Consider taking your number of required grades and then dividing that number by the number of weeks in a grading period and using that to set requirements for your teachers. For example, if you require 27 grades in a nine-week grading period, then set the requirement that teachers enter three grades per week.
- **How and when will grades (and concerns about student performance) be shared with parents and students?** The general rule is the more often the better, but having teachers print out progress reports every time they see students is a bit overkill. Look

for balance between sharing all the time and waiting to let parents or students know about progress until the end of the grading period. If your school has an electronic grading book that parents and students can access, then make getting parent and student access a major priority. Consider a requirement that teachers contact the parents of any student who is failing or close to failing. Require that teachers give some sort of progress report to all students at regular points throughout the grading period.

- **What is the process for changing grades once a grading cycle is over?** Some districts already have a process in place, so you will just be implementing it, but if not then you will want to create a process that is clear, is easy for teachers to do, and has a paper trail.

Once you have established your grading policies, you will develop your practices and procedures. For example, what should progress reports look like? Will there be one type for the whole school or will teachers be able to create their own with certain parameters? When deciding on details like these, keep a few things in mind.

3Ps Apply to All Teachers

You are creating 3Ps for all teachers, from the best of the best who always do everything exactly the way you expect to those who constantly miss deadlines and neglect to enter grades. Your 3Ps need to ensure that the important things get done without being so restrictive that teachers feel as if they're wasting time checking off a list of requirements with no purpose.

You Have to Inspect What You Expect

If you require teachers to turn in three grades by Friday of each week, then you or someone you appoint will have to check on Friday to ensure it has been done. You will also need to establish a consequence for teachers not meeting the expectations. Make sure that whatever you put in place is something you are able to manage.

Be Clear and Straightforward

There is a difference between managing well and micromanaging. In any area for which you have a policy, you need to have practices and procedures to go with it and be able to explain the *why*. If you don't have a why behind one of your 3Ps—or you can't explain it—consider dropping it.

Dropping requirements that have no purpose or have a muddy purpose not only helps alleviate unnecessary work, it also helps reinforce the importance of the requirements that you do keep.

3Ps for Finances

The color of money might be green, but the color of your monetary policy needs to be crystal clear. You may have been hired for your innovative ways to raise student achievement, but one of the quickest ways to get fired or at least find yourself in the headline on the local news is to make a major mistake with the money, whether it's intentional or not. Always remember that it is not your money. It belongs to the school and the students, and it's your job to be the best possible steward of that money.

When first becoming a principal, you need to learn everything you can about the monetary policy of your state and district. Every district is different, and every district has some changes every year, so whether this is your first or twentieth year, staying up to date on financial polices is a must. Contact your supervisor or your district financial representative first for this information. If you do not get the information you need from them, then go to a veteran administrator in your district, preferably someone in your same tier level.

Districts also often send out memos regarding policy changes either electronically or on paper. Learn who the important people are in your district so you will know whose emails or mail to read more closely. Just as an email from you has more weight to a teacher than an email from the football coach, an email you receive from the chief financial officer has more weight than one from the secretary of the athletics director.

Funding Sources and Spending Limitations

Possible sources of money are Title I, other federal funds, state funds, district funds, school bonds, donations, grants, school fund-raisers, PTO/PTA, school vending machines, and advertising and/or yearbook sales. Every district and every school is different; what might be a large source of revenue for one school may not even be a source at all for another.

Many funds have limitations placed on them regarding how they can be spent. For example, Title I funds can only be used for items and purposes that directly impact student education, such as educational materials, tutoring, professional development of staff, and for family engagement. They cannot be used for items that the school is going to sell to raise money. The parents of the school must also vote on whether this money can be used solely for students who are eligible for free or reduced lunch or for all students. Whether a school receives Title I funds and how much depends on the percentage of students in the school who qualify for free or reduced lunch as well as on your district's policies on Title I funds.

Many other funding sources have limitations on what the money can and cannot be spent on. The ability to spend money from grants is often restricted based specifically on the terms of the grant. If you were not involved in the writing or approval of the grant, you need to make sure to review information from the grant provider before approving any funds. If you do not, you may end up approving a purchase that will not be covered by the grant, and the school will then be responsible for the purchase. For example, if a school earns a grant for food for students in need, the school most likely cannot use that money to buy bags to send the food home or to purchase a locking cabinet to keep the food in. When dealing with money, especially money from a grant or another outside source, checking twice and spending once is a wise rule of thumb.

Every district has different policies on money raised by fund-raising. The fair and commonsense thing to do is to ensure that money raised by a particular group belongs to that particular group and is spent only by that group. Nothing will make the faculty and staff question fiscal policy faster than giving money raised by the band to the football team. While there may be times when money goes to a general cause, never raise money under false pretenses. The money should go where it is expected to go and not "disappear" once raised.

Spending Money

The spending of the money can be a complicated process, but you can learn a lot in a short amount of time by consulting with your faculty and staff. Every district is different, so learn your own district's policies. What follows are some general guidelines.

CONSULT DISTRICT PERSONNEL

Review prior audits and ask for areas that have caused concern in the past. The principal might have changed, but the people who do the spending are likely still at the school. Knowing where the school stands in the eyes of the district staff and knowing the fiscal health of the school are key steps in the process.

FIND A MENTOR

This is especially important if fiscal policy is not your strength. You will want to find someone you can trust and who is strong in this area to be your go-to person to answer questions, review your work, and help develop strategies.

Finding someone in the same tier level as you and at a school similar to yours is best. The financial 3Ps of a large high school in an affluent section of town with a highly active and well-funded PTO/PTA will look very different from the 3Ps of a small elementary school in a less affluent area of town with primarily Title I funds to use.

CLEARLY COMMUNICATE YOUR 3Ps

Our recommendation is to put the 3Ps of finance on a one-page document and have every teacher and staff member who might deal with money at any time sign it at the beginning of the year. Make it clear that signing the document means that they have read, understood, and will follow the rules. Then return to them a copy of their signed document.

During the year, if people don't follow the 3Ps and cannot be reimbursed for money they spent or pledged to spend, you can produce a copy of their signed document with the policy they didn't follow highlighted. If at the beginning of the school year you provided clear information for teachers to set them up for success and they choose not to follow the rules, they should be held accountable.

DOCUMENT, DOCUMENT, DOCUMENT

Each district will have its own forms for documenting money and spending, but you may want to create your own tracking system as well to ensure that you know where all of the money has gone and how it got there. This is part of the practices and procedures that you will develop for finances. You can use something as simple as an Excel spreadsheet or more complicated like budget tracking software, as long as it is clear where the money came from and where it went.

You may have a wide variety of accounts in your school, so make sure they are all tracked. We recommend you share your tracking system with everyone on your staff. Printing out the budget on a monthly basis and giving it out to every staff member is a simple way to share this information and keep the color of your fiscal policy crystal clear.

DEVELOP A CUSTOM SYSTEM

You need to have a system you can keep track of—a system that you control and not one that controls you. Think about signing checks, for example. Without a clear system in place, you could spend time every single day signing checks and often have people rushing to get checks signed at the last minute. Instead, establish a simple system. For example: If the requests are in by Monday, they get signed on Thursday. If they are in by Thursday, they get signed on Monday. That way you're only taking time on two days a week to sign things, and you won't be constantly stopped by people asking you to sign their checks. It also helps encourage employees to be organized and forward-thinking. If they know they have to get their requests in by a certain date, they are more likely to get their paperwork done ahead of time rather than late or last minute. The same Monday/Thursday system could be used for requests to use funds as well as any other part of the financial process that you need to review on a regular, continuous basis.

Another easy solution for check signing, money requests, and all other documents that need your signature is to have your bookkeeper create a signing folder. This is one folder that is submitted to you at regular times, with each document bearing a "sign here" sticky note on the line where it needs to be signed. You, of course, will still need to read whatever it is you are signing, but it will save both you and the bookkeeper time if you don't have to search for the line to sign or if the bookkeeper doesn't have to come searching for you because you missed a line.

If you get easily confused by the different financial rules of your district—or by the different names for different steps in the process or different forms that you have to use—consider creating a "cheat sheet." This cheat sheet can be a list of definitions or a flow chart that shows the different steps for requesting money. You could keep this in your office or attach it to the signing folder so it's there when you need it most.

We strongly recommended that you do *not* have a signature stamp that a bookkeeper or other person uses to sign checks, forms, or anything else. If the document is worthy of your signature, then it is worthy of your time to look at it. Allowing others to stamp checks without your oversight can be a sure way to end up in trouble with school finances—which ultimately are your responsibility.

These are simply suggestions, and you may find a variety of other ways that work better, but developing a unique system that you control and that doesn't control you is important in any area of the principalship.

ASK FIRST, SPEND LATER

This should be the policy for you and everyone you are responsible for. In many districts, if money is spent without written permission first, the person who spent it will not be reimbursed for it. Even if that is not the policy in your district, you will want to make sure every dime spent from your limited school budget is spent wisely. If the art teacher goes to the local store and buys crayons for $100, but the school could have ordered them for $50, then this is not a good use of funds. If the teacher had asked first, the money could have been saved or twice as many crayons could have been purchased for the students.

Follow Your 3Ps

Emergency situations will arise where you'll need to act quickly, but as a general rule you will want to always stick to the 3Ps—especially those of your district. If you do not hold your people accountable at the school level, then you will be held accountable for mistakes at the district level.

GET A TRUSTWORTHY BOOKKEEPER

Keeping the financial books is an important part of running a school, but it shouldn't suck up all of your time, so get a quality type A personality to make sure that all of the *i*'s are dotted and *t*'s are crossed. Whether the bookkeeper is someone you hire or someone who has had the job for 20 years, this person needs to be trustworthy, and you need to have confidence in his abilities.

If you do not feel comfortable with the current bookkeeper, you need to have the person removed or moved to another job in the building, one that does not have the same level of responsibility. That way you can find the right person for this important position. But even after you've found the right person, you will still need to closely supervise to ensure that money management is done correctly. All financial decisions are still your responsibility.

3Ps for Employee Relations

Policies concerning employee relations include those about job duties, employee dress, computer access, and attendance, just to name a few. Fiscal policies as described in this chapter are also of significance to employees. This section is not meant to be an exhaustive look at all possible employee-related policies, but rather a focus on general rules to consider.

When creating school-based policies, remember that they cannot contradict local, state, or federal rules, and the expectations for one policy cannot contradict another policy. For example, if the district contract with teachers stipulates that they are required to be at school 20 minutes prior to the school day and stay until 20 minutes after the school day, you cannot require teachers to arrive 30 minutes prior and stay 30 minutes after.

Employee attendance is one of the most important areas to set up clear, detailed 3Ps. With so many people in confined quarters, germs are bound to spread and employees will get sick. Ideally the majority of employees won't be absent frequently, but when they are, they leave lesson plans for substitute teachers to follow. You may be entering a school where some employees are absent often and don't leave lesson plans.

You can put policies in place to help with these situations. First, implement a system for letting the school know of a pending absence and requesting a substitute. This may be a system from the district, a school-based system, or a combination of the two, but the more notice you're given of the pending absence, the better prepared you can be.

Second, create a system for getting lesson plans and rosters to the substitute teacher. Generally this is the responsibility of the teacher for any planned absence. But *where* the plans are left can often be as important as *whether* they are left. If the teacher leaves everything in a binder in the bottom desk drawer but no one is aware of that, then the plans might as well not exist. Keeping the plans in a central location or having "hallway buddies" can help. Hallway buddies are teachers on the same hall who either have a copy of their buddy's plans and rosters or know where the teacher keeps them.

Sometimes absences come up unexpectedly and the teacher cannot provide lesson plans for the day. If you require teachers to submit emergency lesson plans at the beginning of the year, they'll be available when needed. It's disruptive to student learning when teachers are absent, but expecting perfect attendance is not realistic. Having policies, practices, and procedures in place can make the unavoidable less disrupting.

To ensure that occasional absences don't turn into chronic absences, you may want to track the attendance of teachers. You can use a simple format like a one-page sheet that lists the months of the school year where you can mark who is absent each day and why. If you notice that a certain teacher calls in sick every Monday for a month, use your tracking system as a jumping off point for a conversation with the teacher and, if necessary, further investigation into the matter. Frequent absences might be a sign of having too much fun over the weekend or a weekly doctor's appointment for a chronic illness. Obviously, these two situations warrant very different responses.

Some principals require teachers to contact them directly if they are going to be absent. The rationale for this "old-fashioned" policy is that people usually think twice about being absent if they have to talk in person to their supervisor. If you decide to use this system, you will want to track not only who calls you and how often, but also anyone who does not call as required. You can follow up with them as needed.

3Ps for Emergencies and Other Contingencies

One of the "exciting" parts of running a school is that with so many students, parents, and employees, strange things happen. Some of these may be a danger to children, which is when contingency plans are most critical. Other situations are merely inconvenient, unexpected, or just unusual, but it's still important to have thought out what to do.

Contingencies are sometimes related to the age level or community a school serves or even the building the school is housed in. For example, what happens if the power goes out? In a school with plenty of natural light, this may not be an issue. But in a school with classrooms that lack windows, this can be a major problem. The age of the students will affect the plan in this situation as well. Another example is a school that is prone to leaking or flooding. What follows are just a few of the possible emergencies and contingencies that you may need to consider.

Planned Student Disruptions

Occasionally, teachers and administrators hear rumors of a fight, demonstration, prank, or other disruption planned by students. An easy way to stop these events is to change the dismissal plan without the students' knowledge using the "door knocker plan." If you know something is going to happen after school, and dismissal is normally at 2:30p.m., assign teachers to certain hallways to knock on doors to dismiss students one class at a time. It is easy to do several hallways at a time, and the unconventional dismissal is often enough to stop any planned disruption from occurring.

Parent Disruptions and Confrontations

Sometimes families are the cause of the disruption. Parents who confront the children of other parents have the potential to be dangerous. This is why every school needs a structured sign-in/sign-out protocol so parents do not have unsupervised access to children at the school. If a parent tries to confront a child, that parent must be stopped. Tell the parent the behavior is unacceptable and will not be tolerated, and follow up in writing. If necessary, the school resource officer or local police may need to be involved.

Occasionally parents confront other parents, perhaps in an effort to defend their child from a perceived bullying situation. When parents confront one another at school or school events over the behavior of their children, you must immediately intervene. This type of disruption can easily ruin a school event.

Typically, the parents will want to work out their concerns then and there, but you're better off escorting them off the property. When emotions are high, you are unlikely to make any progress toward resolving the issue. Keep the families separated and schedule a time to meet separately with them the following day to resolve the concern.

Parking at School Events

Elementary school parties are often widely attended, and parking can become hazardous. Try to time parties or events so that only one grade level is celebrating at a time. This makes the parking crunch less pronounced and allows parents of multiple siblings to celebrate with both or all of their children. If you can work with school neighbors to identify satellite locations for parking during these circumstances, it will be appreciated by those parents in attendance and those businesses and residences that neighbor the school.

Death of a Student

Of the many things that principals encounter in their careers, nothing is as tragic as the death of a student. Whether the death was caused by an accident, terminal illness, or a crime, handle these unfortunate events consistently and keep the unique aspects of the school and the school community in mind. What is appropriate in a small rural school, where high school students have been together since elementary school, may not be appropriate in a large urban high school with a high mobility rate.

A crisis team may be needed if many students and staff are grieving. Crisis teams are often developed by deploying several counselors from the school district or elsewhere. While it is helpful to have numbers on your side in dealing with a crisis, it isn't always best to have strangers assist for the day. In smaller communities, it is helpful to have counselors from the feeder schools assist since many of the students would have known them in their younger years. However, much of the time you'll redeploy resources from within the school, which will mean that everyone is on crisis management duty.

The best people to help students through a crisis are staff members the students have a rapport with. So if a student comes to her math teacher for help in a crisis, the math teacher ought to do what he can to meet the needs of his student—even if he needs to get direction from a counselor.

Events surrounding some deaths present specific challenges. For example, a high school student who is killed in an armed robbery presents a very different situation from a student who succumbs to a deadly disease. Be careful not to treat one death as more appropriate or tragic than another. Even if a student's own actions led to the student's death, avoid vilifying or judging. Your role is to support those who are left behind.

Stories from the Field

A principal learned about a suicide attempt that occurred in the middle of

> the night. The principal talked to the student's mom from the hospital, and she confided that death was imminent. By morning, news of the attempted suicide had spread among the student body via text message, and many students had a strong emotional response. The principal called a faculty meeting 30 minutes before school started and explained what had happened, including the impending death. She laid out a strategy for handling the students' outpouring of grief, and teachers had a few minutes to process the crisis before leading students through it. The principal asked the teachers to supervise the students coming into the building, help maintain normalcy, and identify students who may need individual support. Those students were given one-on-one support while others continued on with their regular school day.

Sharing the information as it became available and allowing teachers to gather themselves emotionally before facing students were critical steps in managing this crisis.

Death of a Staff Member

The impact of a staff member's death can vary depending on the staff member's relationship with students, the size of the school, the age of the staff member, and the circumstances of the death. It is important to allow children to grieve but without demanding that they do—a tightrope that can be difficult to navigate.

While you likely don't need a standing policy for recognizing the life and death of a staff member, some sort of tribute or gesture can be helpful to children (and adults) as they process their grief. A tree-planting ceremony, the naming of a section of the school, or hosting a book or coat drive in the deceased teacher's memory are often positive ways to allow children to honor the teacher and channel their grief into a project that helps bring closure to the loss.

Children Stranded at School

Every now and then, bad weather or a natural disaster such as an earthquake will leave students at school without a way home because their parents are stuck in traffic or otherwise unable to get to the school. When this happens, you are responsible for those students. The first thing to do is get assistance. In these scenarios, many staff members will be compelled to leave to get home for their own children. However, usually some staff members will volunteer to stay.

Gathering these people is critical to help reduce the adult-to-child ratio.

The second thing is to figure out how much food is available. Cafeterias typically maintain some ready-to-eat "emergency rations" for situations like this. If this is not the practice at your school, establish it as one. Once supervision and snacks are worked out, organize recreational activities to keep students meaningfully engaged until the crisis is over.

Establish a procedure to address these situations even if you are out of the building when the crisis occurs. The key factor in developing these plans is making sure they can be uniformly instituted.

On a smaller scale, sometimes a bus will return with one or more elementary students if their parents were not at the bus stop to pick them up, or sometimes an incident will happen on a bus requiring the bus driver to return to school for disciplinary action. In this case, it's up to you to find a way for the student to get home. If no one is available to pick up the student, does the school have a plan for how the student gets home? Is there written policy on staff driving the student home? Are emergency contact numbers updated on a regular basis for students? If your school doesn't have an answer to these questions, then you'll need to establish a plan. An unattended child is the responsibility of the school until the student can be delivered home.

Depending on the specific rules for the district and/or school, you may be allowed to let a staff member drive a student home. If the family grants permission over the phone, it is wise for staff members to email you stating that permission was granted to drive the student home, who they talked to, and when they talked to the person. This provides some safeguards for the staff member.

Imminent Dangerous Weather

Tornadoes and flash flooding can create an immediate need for a student body to take cover. This is also a time when some parents feel compelled to pick up their children. In this situation, offer parents shelter, but if the school is operating under a weather-related crisis, you cannot devote resources to looking up students' schedules so their parents can leave with them. Reassure parents that their child is safe and that once the weather system has passed, normal dismissal procedures will be reinstated.

Massive Student Early Dismissals

When a tragedy or major event occurs, parents often want to be with their children and will want to take them out of school. While this may not be educationally sound or necessary, it is usually best to allow it, excuse the absence or early dismissal, and let the parents process the event at home as they see fit.

Parent Concerns or Complaints

Parents do not just share a school community with one another. Children who are friends are often the springboard for parents to become friends. Families see each other at scout meetings and ballgames as well as in the neighborhoods. Sometimes families band together to support or oppose a policy of yours, or they develop a complaint about a teacher or program. And sometimes these groups will request a meeting with you.

While a group meeting can be more time-efficient, it is rarely more effective than meeting with the concerned families individually. When a group of parents meets with the principal, some individuals are compelled to be present to see what is going on rather than because they have firsthand knowledge or true concern of the issue. Instead, set up individual meetings with each family so that only those who truly have a complaint will come forward. Individual meetings also show that you believe the issue is important enough to take this time, and they allow you to develop relationships with the parents.

Parents Demanding a Different Teacher

Of all the requests parents make of principals, the dreaded "switch the teacher" request is filled with land mines. The biggest problem occurs when you have teachers whose classrooms many parents want their children removed from and others who are wildly popular, resulting in more requests than can be accommodated. Teacher A cannot teach zero students while teacher B teaches twice the capacity a classroom can hold!

The best solution is to engage the parent in a discussion about what the child's needs are and focus the conversation on the child, not on the teacher. Have a policy that you will not take teacher requests but will commit to matching children with teachers who can best meet their needs. That way, parents can specify what they are looking for. Often, a request for a teacher is based on what a parent heard about the teacher, which isn't necessarily accurate. Some teachers are popular because they are excellent; but popularity does not always stem from excellence. By explaining to parents that placements are made based on student needs, you direct the conversation so that the parent has expertise and provides valued input rather than simply requesting teacher A because everyone in the neighborhood says that teacher A is a better teacher than teacher B.

When a parent demands that a student be removed from a teacher's class, the situation is usually complex. The best recourse in this situation is to bring everyone to the table—parents, student, teacher, and principal—to talk about the family's concerns. Develop a plan to address these concerns, and follow up with the family on a weekly basis to ensure they don't feel abandoned.

If a parent has genuine concerns about teacher performance that requires remediation, you'll want to address those with the teacher in the absence of the parent. If you're supportive of the teacher, he is more likely to work to meet the student's or parent's requests. However, when teachers do not feel your support, they may become defensive and try to protect themselves rather than work to fix the situation.

Stories from the Field

A fourth grader became highly anxious and his parents began to question him about what was occurring in school. He explained that his teacher had a magic hat that looked like a reflective visor. When she wore that hat, she was "out of the office" and students were not allowed to ask her questions. This caused

a great deal of stress for the child, who sought confirmation about his work during seat time. The student also revealed that the teacher had a notebook in which students wrote down transgressions of other students that the teacher reviewed daily so no one had to "tattle" on anyone else. The fourth grader began imagining that the book was full of submissions about him, increasing his anxiety.

The parents demanded that the child be removed, and the principal and teacher met with the parents. The parents were not impressed with the teacher's explanations and reassurances that their child had nothing to fear. The principal did not move the child, but made a promise to follow up with the child individually on a weekly basis for the next month. After each of these checkups, the principal contacted the parents to summarize what the child said. These frequent contacts helped reassure the parents that the principal was closely monitoring their concerns.

The principal also made a point to check in with the child. Since the principal's office can seem intimidating, she sought out the child during lunch a few times per month to see what his perceptions were. Having this regular monitoring helped decrease the student's anxiety, which also helped put the parents at ease.

This scenario highlights a major problem principals have when they must tell a parent (or any stakeholder) no. The principal did not say, "I won't change teachers. Case closed." Instead, she communicated a belief that although the answer was no, she was concerned and committed to developing a solution, and she would continue to play an active role with the student and teacher. By following through with the weekly checkups, the principal reassured the parents that she was partnering with them in the education of their child.

3Ps for the Day-to-Day

While it is the emergencies and random events that will stick out in your memory, it is the day-to-day life that can make or break you. You could raise test scores and improve teacher morale, but the moment a pep rally turns into a mass fight or a kindergartner gets left in the school building by herself, all the good is forgotten. While some of the basics of the day-to-day may seem simple or obvious, in order to ensure that things run smoothly, you need to have policies, practices, and procedures in place for even the most routine events.

When creating these 3Ps, consider school from the perspective of a student from the beginning to the end of the day. What is being done to supervise the student, to ensure the student is getting a quality education, and to ensure the student feels safe and secure and taken care of? Keeping these thoughts in mind can help you create policies that work for the students in your school. As with any policy, an accountability plan must be built into the system to ensure that it works effectively.

Stories from the Field

A first-year administrative team in their newly assigned school had put many policies and procedures in place to deal with student arrival, class change, and dismissal, and behavior incidents during these times had begun to drop. An outside agency requested the school allow an off-campus group to give a presentation to the freshman class. The group leaders said they had everything planned and would run the program. The principal trusted them and did not involve many of his own staff in the event. Everything went well until the program finished early. To fill up the extra time, the group played a popular

> song that contained inappropriate language and references to activities that are not encouraged in the school environment. Students were dismissed and left en masse, being boisterous and disruptive. They were not prepared to go to their next classes, and teachers had to settle them down and remind them of appropriate behavior expectations.

This encounter emphasizes a valuable lesson: It is *your* building and school. Even when an outside speaker or group comes in, it is still your school and your responsibility to ensure everything goes well. There is never any downtime as long as students are in the building.

The beginning and end of the school day, along with the various normal school events, are often when stakeholders, most notably parents, come to the school and see the behavior of the students, faculty, and staff. It is important that these interactions are positive ones, and that the school is running smoothly and purposefully at those times. If a parent asks a question about where car rider pick-up is or how students know which bus to ride, members of the staff should be able to answer those questions or know who the correct person is to answer the questions. If policies, practices, and procedures are consistent, you're likely to have fewer problems. That will lead not only to a better environment, but also to a better perception in the community of that environment.

Arrival and Dismissal

Arrival and dismissal will look different depending on whether your school is an elementary, middle, or high school, and whether the majority of students are bus riders, walkers, or car riders. In order to ensure smooth transitions at the beginning and end of the day, establish an orderly and safe traffic flow for students and place staff at strategic locations to help guide them. The neighborhood around the school will appreciate an orderly plan for these times, too!

With elementary school students, staff often need to help young students get in and out of cars and buses safely and quickly to keep traffic moving through the property. These times are an excellent opportunity for you to be visible and seen as the leader of the school. Your presence also verifies the importance of these activities and holds other staff members who are assigned arrival/dismissal duties accountable.

Stories from the Field

The majority of students at an elementary school arrived by car, with parents parking in the neighborhood and walking their children to school in order

to avoid having to wait in long traffic lines. Neighbors were upset about cars parking on their streets and blocking driveways. To add to the congestion, parents of the youngest children were walking their students all the way to their classrooms. These students were having a hard time transitioning and starting their school day. Crying students and lingering parents often caused kindergarten classes to start late.

To deal with the traffic problem, the principal arranged for teachers, staff, and administrators to work the bus and car arrival lines. This duty was essential for safety to make sure no children were running or exiting cars into moving traffic. Cars were motioned forward to fill up the available car lanes, and when the cars were stopped and the lanes were full, a teacher blew a whistle to signal children to exit cars. The staff assisted the students as necessary. When all cars had been unloaded and students were clear of the lanes, a signal was made from staff positioned throughout the drop-off area, and another whistle was blown signaling cars to move again. This routine was repeated until the beginning of the official start time of school. The

> staff presence enabled parents to stay in the car, which sped up the drop-off time.
>
> To help the transition for the kindergartners and their parents, the school established an "Independence Day" when parents were encouraged to let their children out of the car or say good-bye at the school doors. Other staff members were assigned specific stations in and out of the building to help get students inside and on their way to class and to comfort any students struggling with the transition.

By dealing specifically with the two problems that were causing the most congestion in the morning, the school was able to improve the traffic flow while ensuring a safe, orderly environment that was more conducive to learning. Often, many of the issues that exist for arrival will exist for dismissal as well; therefore, the same procedures will generally work. If they do not, then figure out the specific problems and develop solutions tailored to them.

High school and middle school arrivals and dismissals pose different challenges, but the solution and policy are essentially the same as elementary school: staff supervision of children. In high school, you might have bus riders, walkers, car riders, and student drivers. The student parking lot needs teacher supervision during arrival and dismissal in order to ensure that teenage drivers are practicing safe driving techniques and students are not congregating, causing traffic congestion, or violating school rules. With staff present encouraging students to get out of or into their cars, potential problems can be alleviated. You will need to create specific procedures and practices that work for your school design and supervision needs.

You'll need to have a procedure for late arrivals and early dismissals as well. Establish a specific location for sign-ins and sign-outs that is close to the front of the school so parents do not have to walk around the building to pick up their child. It is also important to document late arrivals and early dismissals. Ensure that students only leave with appropriate adults.

Address a student's frequent tardiness or early dismissals with parents. These absences can have a negative impact on student learning and success. Many school districts have an escalation policy for addressing tardiness, with the classroom teacher making the first contact to parents, then the school office making contact via a letter documenting the tardiness, and finally, if not corrected, central office personnel working with parents to correct the issue.

Between Class Transitions

Making sure students don't get "lost" between classes requires the efforts of the whole school. The more supervision in place, the fewer problems you'll have. Assign posts of duty to all adults in the building during these transition times, encouraging students to get to their locations in a timely manner. At elementary schools, friendliness with students is often a given, but too often at the upper levels, we forget that asking with a smile is far more effective than telling with a frown.

Create a simple spreadsheet to track who is supposed to be at each post and when. This helps your personnel know where to be and is also an important form of accountability, making it easy for you to see when teachers are not at their posts so you can follow up with them. This communicates the message that everyone has a part in making sure students are attending school in a safe and orderly environment.

Lunch

No matter the structure your school has for lunch, there are a few universal critical details. First, food needs to be available to all students. Second, teachers must have a lunch break as well. Third, as with all day-to-day aspects, make sure all students are supervised at all times.

When making a lunch plan, don't be afraid to think outside the box—or the lunchroom. Who, other than teachers, can supervise students during lunch? Is it possible for teachers to get their allotted lunchtime while still taking part in the supervision of lunch? Do all students need to sit in the cafeteria during lunchtime? Can lunchtime be a time for eating as well as other things, like participating in clubs or tutoring? Think about the particular students in the building and their needs, and develop a lunch plan that works for your school.

Recess

While an elementary school principal might not have to directly supervise recess on a daily basis, you will want to establish procedures for student supervision.

> ### Stories from the Field
>
> **A new elementary school principal noticed that many students were coming to the office for injuries sustained on the playground during recess. To find out more, he observed the playground during one of the grade-level recess times. He noticed that the students were running around, playing on the playground as children do, while the grade-level teachers all grouped together in one spot talking. The school had established playground expectations, but teachers were not enforcing these expectations or adequately supervising them. The principal followed up by observing other**

> grade-level recess times and found the same to be true.
>
> The principal met with teachers and reviewed the school's playground expectations. He asked teachers to review these with the students. Since the students were spread out over a pretty wide area during recess, he assigned pairs of teachers specific spots to monitor. Either he or his assistant made rounds to ensure teachers were in their designated spots. With the increased adult supervision, student accidents and injuries decreased.

The new principal in this scenario did not jump to conclusions and did not punish the teachers. Instead, he took time to observe what was happening and then made adjustments that were best for students. While the teachers probably preferred all talking together, placing them in pairs allowed them some of the adult interaction they craved, but not at the expense of the children's safety and security.

The principal also exemplified two important points:

1. **Don't punish for what has not been taught.** Since this principal had not yet taken the time to review with teachers or students the expectations of behavior on the playground, it would have been unfair

of him to punish either group for their behavior. But now that expectations have been clearly established, he can begin to hold individuals accountable for their actions.
2. **Inspect what you expect.** If the principal wants teachers to follow through with his request, he must follow through as well. Regular monitoring shows teachers, students, and parents that he values the safety of students and is mindful of his responsibility in providing a safe and secure environment.

Regular School Events

Many school activities and events occur regularly though not daily, such as tests, assemblies, and pep rallies. Since these situations are less frequent, it can be easy for those involved to forget what the 3Ps are for them. Thus, it is important to have easy ways to share information about such events whenever needed. If you have four pep rallies a year, communicate directions, teacher responsibilities, and other details four times a year as well. Don't assume people will remember (or just know) what to do.

Test Administration

With school administration of the ACT or SAT, state-mandated end-of-year testing, other state-mandated tests, benchmark assessments, and initial assessments to determine the needs of students, testing and test administration are now a regular part of doing business in public schools. That testing may be done with pencil and bubble sheet or electronically with computer and mouse.

Regardless of whether you agree with the merits of testing, you are responsible for ensuring that all testing is done correctly and that students are provided a test-friendly environment. Clearly state expectations about test security, integrity, and environment. You may not be the main test coordinator in the building, but as with everything else, ultimately you are responsible.

TESTING SECURITY

Districts and states often have testing security rules in place for state-mandated tests, and in many states, breaking any of them is grounds for firing. Make sure you have a clear understanding of those rules and that everyone involved in testing also understands them. You may want to have all testing staff sign a document stating that they understand.

Keep testing materials secure and establish policies for documenting that the materials have arrived at the school, which materials have been used, and what materials are sent back for scoring. You also need a way to track who has access to the materials at any given time. Place the tests in a location that can be locked and where you know who has access. Create a simple log sheet for people to sign in and out the materials, with a column to mark the quantity. If the test is electronic, it may be passcodes and log-in instructions that need to be kept secure. If that information is delivered via email, specify in the email with whom the information can and cannot be shared.

TESTING INTEGRITY

Testing integrity is as important as—if not more important than—testing security. Testing security means nothing if teachers are previewing the materials and teaching their students specific problems they find in the tests or giving out answers during the test. These are both cheating. Though it may seem obvious, be specific with teachers that this type of behavior is not allowed, and follow up when you suspect or know of such activities. Limit the temptation for teachers by keeping all materials locked up, not giving out access codes to the test until the day of the test, or having teachers administer tests to a grade or subject level other than their own.

If you do have a breach of integrity and you try to sweep it under the rug, someone will eventually stumble on the bulge on the floor and discover the truth. You will look worse than if you had been forthcoming in the beginning. Sometimes honest mistakes happen with testing, and tests are given in an inappropriate way or a particular rule is not followed. This too needs to be dealt with immediately so a mistake does not look like it was intentional. Self-reporting is always the best type of reporting. All states and districts will have detailed procedures for reporting testing irregularities or violations.

TESTING ENVIRONMENT

Think about all aspects of the test and plan exactly what needs to be done to help cut down on confusion, wasted time, and a disorderly environment. Following are some questions you or your testing coordinator will want to consider when preparing for testing:

- **How many students can or should be in one testing environment?** Generally, the fewer the better, but every testing room must be supervised by an adult. Therefore, you will have to look at the number of students testing, the number of adults supervising, the number of possible locations, and the number of seats and/or computers available in each location to determine what will work best.
- **Where will the testing environment(s) be?** This will be determined by what group of students is testing, what locations are available for testing, what is needed in the testing environment, and what else will be going on at the same time. For example, if only 25 percent of the students in the school are testing, and testing will go into the

lunchtime of other students, then it is not a good idea to put the testing students in a room on the same hallway as the cafeteria. In general, it is best to have testing students in a location where outside distractions can be minimized.

- **How will students get to and from the testing environment?** As with any student transition time, having well-informed adults supervise is the best way to ensure success.
- **How will students be separated into various testing environments?** Options include separating by last name, by class, by grade level, and so on. If the tests or test access codes come from an outside organization or are separated in a specific manner such as by last name or class, then this will affect how students are separated. Otherwise figure out what system will work best for your testing situation.
- **Which adults will administer the test to which students?** As a general rule, don't have teachers administer high-stakes tests to the students in their own class. This reduces the possibility that teachers might try to give inappropriate help to their students. Only certified employees should administer tests and have access to the testing materials, so

don't use parents or others from the community.
- **How will the adults administering the test be trained?** It is a good idea to train test administrators in person, but when that isn't possible, online training or sending instructions by email is an acceptable option. The best solution is to train in person and follow up by sending out the directions in an email. If the test is computer based, take the adults into a computer lab and have them go through as much of the log-in process as possible, so they can see what it will look like for students and be better able to troubleshoot problems. This type of testing, because it is newer, may be the least familiar for all involved, so more preparation is likely needed.
- **What is the procedure for handing out and getting back testing materials?** Make a list of testing administrators and the quantity of tests or access codes each administrator needs. When testing administrators pick up their materials, have them count them and sign for them, and have them count them and sign them back in when they return the materials.
- **What will be the procedure for administering the test?** For state and

national tests, this information is given to you. We recommend using some of those procedures for your own tests as well to help students be prepared for those higher stakes tests.

- **What will the adult administering the test do if there is a problem or an emergency?** Make sure the adult can contact the test coordinator. If possible, make the coordinator available by phone to answer questions and deal with emergencies, and have test administrators use classroom phones or cell phones to call. Alternatively, put the coordinator in a central location near the testing rooms and have runners in the hallway who can quickly get to the coordinator and back to the testing rooms. Having a list of common problems with recommended solutions can also help reduce issues and confusion during testing.
- **What special accommodations need to be made for students with disabilities or students who are English language learners?** Generally, this is clearly specified by the state and district, so follow those directions carefully. Students' IEPs may also specify testing accommodations.
- **How long will the test be? Does the daily schedule need to be altered**

because of the test? Will it affect lunch for the students?** Some tests have required sets of time, while others do not. If the test does not have a set time, then you will need to estimate how long the test will take in order to make plans. If it is a yearly test, track how long the tests take each year so you know how long to plan for. The number of students involved as well as the length of the test will determine what alterations need to be made to the schedule.

- **Will the students or adults need breaks? If so, how will that be coordinated?** If it is a 45-minute test, then breaks most likely will not be needed, but if it is a four-hour test, then breaks will be needed for students and adults. For students, set breaks at specific times and try to keep the disruption to testing at a minimum. For adults, assign extra adults to relieve administrators at specific times.
- **What, if any, incentives will be given to students for full effort on the test?** Whether it is extra recess time, a special assembly, a school wristband, or a T-shirt, incentives can be a great way to encourage students who may not be intrinsically motivated to do well on tests. Consider the importance of the test, the money and time

available, and the grade level of the students when determining whether to provide incentives and what incentives to provide.
- **What is the plan in classes after testing?** Students are generally either worn out from the intensity of testing or wound up from having to sit quietly for so long. Plans for the rest of the school day should take this into account and either allow time for students to reflect on their testing experience or engage in a hands-on activity.

Sitting quietly working and focusing only on oneself is not a natural behavior for a child or teenager, or even most adults, so take the time to teach students proper testing behavior explicitly and repeatedly, starting ahead of the first time they take any sort of assessment. Consider posting testing expectations in all classes and having all teachers and administrators enforce them.

Celebrations

There is a fine balance between classroom celebrations that help build relationships, improve climate, and have educational value and those that distract from student achievement. It's up to you to set the expectations for celebrations.

Stories from the Field

An experienced principal moved to a new elementary school in a new district. Almost immediately upon her appointment, teachers and the parent-teacher organization wanted to know what she would allow in the way of class celebrations. Teachers listed Johnny Appleseed Day, Halloween, winter celebrations, Valentine's Day, St. Patrick's Day, President's Day, Black History Month, and several others as occasions they felt should be celebrated. The principal reviewed the handbook from the district and saw that class parties were not allowed, and class celebrations were limited to two per year. She reiterated this policy to the teachers, pointing out that all celebrations should have an instructional focus (keeping them from being "parties"). Teachers asked for clarification. The principal stated that celebrations should not interfere with instruction, but she understood the importance of building classroom culture—and that celebrations could help with that. For example, building gingerbread houses before winter break could be a lesson in geometric designs.

She soon realized that some teachers exceeded the two celebrations per year by claiming that their celebrations were

> actually lessons. One teacher held several celebrations to mark holidays around the world, saying these were part of the social studies standards she was covering.

In this situation, the teachers and parents were trying to take advantage of the fact that the principal was new to the school and district in order to get some leeway with class celebrations. To avoid such situations, work with teachers to develop celebrations that are fun but also have instructional merit. For example, celebrations might include student projects and culminate in a day of shared learning. Research shows that project-based learning has instructional merit for students.

By training teachers in this or another appropriate method, and even helping develop curriculum, you help turn what initially might be nothing more than glorified class parties into genuine learning experiences for students where appropriate grade-level curriculum standards are taught. You move beyond being an administrator to a true instructional leader.

If there is not a district level policy, then we recommend creating your own, remembering that student learning is the focus of school. Parties for the sake of just having a party really do not have a place in the school day, but engaging lessons that are fun and educational at the same time are always welcome.

Pep Rallies and Other Large Student Body Events

To have successful pep rallies and other events with a large group of students, make a plan ahead of time and make sure all staff members know their responsibilities. Student supervision is critical, so you may want to create a map of the event location showing where all students and adults are to be located, along with descriptions of the adult responsibilities in each location. Post administrators in strategic locations so one of them can get anywhere one is needed in a short amount of time.

Depending on the age of the students and their experience with different types of events, the students may also need to be taught how to behave. Establish general rules about behavior at pep rallies and other events, and make your expectations clear. Review rules and expectations before every event to keep them fresh in the minds of even the youngest and most squirrelly of students.

Entering and exiting are key times when things can go wrong, so put plans in place for these times as well. To avoid having a large group of students coming in at once through limited doorways, invite them in groups, such as one hallway at a time. Have teachers escort their classes, and if possible have different entrance and exit points for students coming from different sections of the building. As always, have supervision in place before the first student walks in.

Bored students are unhappy students, so try to make any event fun and interesting for students. The more students are involved and the more interesting things there are to see, the more likely it is that all will have a good experience.

Sporting Events

Sporting events are the most common time that you have a mixture of students, parents, and community members. Not only is it harder to control larger groups, but you are also responsible for the safety and well-being of people whose behavior you cannot dictate in the way you can with students. Not surprisingly, strict supervision is key in this situation as well.

> ### Stories from the Field
>
> **A high school had low attendance at its football games, and the few students who did attend were not allowed to stand and cheer for the team. Administrators patrolled the walkways around the stadium instructing students to remain in the stands. Even the game announcer reminded students to sit down in between calling plays. The game**

> **resembled a controlled testing environment without the tests.**

This sort of super-regulated environment is sometimes enforced in schools with histories of discipline problems or in schools with new or inexperienced principals who think that strict control is the only way to ensure an orderly environment. But there is a difference between supervising and being overly strict. Supervision keeps problems from starting, but over-restriction can cause them. Instead of going to such an extreme, consider doing the following:

- Adjust traffic flows during the games to make sure there are walkways for people to move about the stadium.
- Create a student section where students can stand and cheer without blocking the view of other spectators.
- Provide opportunities for students to be involved at games.

***

No matter the situation, the more prepared you are the better. Having policies, practices, and procedures in place is an absolute must for a well-run school. They help create a well-organized, predictable environment, which is the most conducive for learning. Taking the time early on to get 3Ps in place frees you up later to truly focus on instructional leadership.

CHAPTER FOUR

Encouraging Teamwork and Camaraderie

A principal works with all types of teachers, from the bright-eyed, idealistic, 22-year-old, first-year teacher to the 30-year veteran who has seen and heard it all. You'll have Pollyannas who face each day with a smile and can-do attitude, Negative Neds who can always find something to complain about, and everyone in between. There will be the rock star teachers who engage every student in learning and the rocks who don't do much of anything at all.

This chapter provides some basic practices that will help you support and develop all teachers. While the focus of this and the next two chapters is on teachers, these same principles can be applied to other staff members as well.

Create a Culture Where People Feel Welcomed

Teachers perform their best when they feel welcome from the moment they walk into a school for the first time—and keep on feeling welcome every day, even after 30 years. That kind of atmosphere doesn't happen by accident. As principal, it's up to you to create it and encourage all administrative staff, teacher leaders, and everyone in the building to carry it out.

Modeling is generally the best way to create such a culture. Never underestimate the power of a smile, a hello, or remembering to ask about a teacher's sick child. In addition, put people who have warm, caring, and understanding personalities in key positions that interact with people new to the building.

Planning fun events for staff—and including members of the staff in the coordination process—is another way to create a welcoming culture. Nearly every staff will have its natural party planners who love social gatherings and enjoy being involved in the process of putting together such events. Enlist those people to create a morale committee or sunshine committee that plans fun events such as celebrations of staff birthdays. This group can also organize snacks at meetings and support for faculty members who have had a baby or suffered a loss. You may provide school funds, approve all final committee decisions, or regularly check up on the plans, but you don't have to be actively involved in every detail to show that you think building and maintaining positive morale is important.

Create a Culture Where Teachers Feel Valued

Teachers are professionals who have invested in perfecting their craft and understandably want to be treated that way. While all your decisions won't always make all teachers happy, you can take steps to help teachers feel as if they are valued. Recognizing teachers specifically for work they do or celebrating teachers as a whole are both ways to create such a culture.

The following are some low-cost ways to recognize teachers.

Weekly Certificates of Appreciation

Create a nomination process through which faculty and staff can nominate a coworker for excellent work or going above and beyond. For example, creating a highly engaging lesson for students, helping out a fellow colleague, or planning a parent engagement event. Establish a small committee of teachers and administrators to choose the weekly winner. Deliver the certificate to the winner and take a few minutes to explain why he was chosen. Take a picture of the person with the certificate. Post the photo in the school, include it in the school paper or newsletter, or email it out—a simple process that only costs the paper to print the certificate.

Though the process is simple, if not done consistently, it can quickly become a point of contention rather than the positive experience it's meant to be. For each step of the process (due date for nominations, due date for voting, a time to print the certificate, and a time to deliver it), add a reminder on the master calendar to help everyone stay on top of it. This can help keep the process going even on a busy week, and if it falls by the wayside for a day or two, it can easily be restarted. As with anything you try, a momentary stumble should not mean the end of the race.

Awards for Extra Work Done

These could be simple certificates or even little trophies or plaques with sayings such as "Thanks for that extra Burro kick" (if your school mascot is a burro), "Way to BEE amazing" (if it's a bee or yellow jacket), or "Way to soar above the crowd" (if it's an eagle). You can give this award whenever teachers have gone above and beyond the call of duty, perhaps helping a student in need, directing the school play, or volunteering for every family engagement event. It is a simple yet effective way to let teachers know that you noticed their extra work, and it also encourages them to put forth such effort again in the future.

The cost for this will depend on what type of gift you choose for the teacher. But the value of this award is contained in the sentiment behind it, not the price of the gift. Teachers appreciate being noticed for their hard work, and the physical gift just serves as a reminder of the appreciation.

Holiday Bonuses

Most schools do not have the money to buy holiday presents for every teacher, and unlike what sometimes happens in the corporate world, a bonus check is not waiting for all who have worked hard during the year. But you can award your own "holiday bonus" to the staff. This is a certificate from you to each staff member thanking that person for something specific. The "bonus" is the personalized thank you that you give. Since most teachers have limited interaction time with you, this is a nice way to make a personal connection.

Here are a few helpful suggestions for giving out "holiday bonuses."

- **Start early.** This is especially true if your staff is large. While creating certificates for 10 or 20 teachers is not very time-consuming, the same cannot be said for creating them for 100 or more. Also, since the value of these bonuses is tied to the personal investment you put into them, the task of formatting the certificates or printing them cannot be farmed out to someone else, and for some principals, this can take more time than for others.

- **Keep track of what you write for each person each year.** The idea of a personalized message loses its sincerity when more than one person gets the exact same one. Invariably you will have more to say about a teacher you've worked with more closely or are highly impressed with, but you should still take the time to think of something specific and sincere for those teachers you don't know as well or regard as highly. Also, if a teacher receives the exact same certificate two years in a row, it can give the impression that the certificate is something you do because you feel obligated rather than because you truly mean it. Keeping a list that you can refer to each year will prevent duplications.
- **Don't leave out anyone.** Your list can help with this, too. Whether you hand out the certificates individually or give them out in front of the entire staff as a part of the fall semester wrap-up, it's essential not to leave out anyone. Make sure your list is up-to-date, and compare it to the number of certificates you've written to keep this simple and benign error from upsetting the person who is accidently overlooked.

October Ooze

As a way to get all your teachers involved in helping each other feel valued, assign every teacher a peer to write an "October Ooze" note. The note begins with, "We are oozing with good cheer because (teacher's name)..." The writer then writes about the great attributes of the teacher or lists positive things the teacher has contributed to the school. Designate someone to coordinate the "October Ooze"—handing out "ooze assignments" for everyone and overseeing the process to ensure that all "oozes" are appropriately positive, focused on what each teacher adds to the school, and distributed in a timely manner. Once again, it is important to ensure that everyone receives one.

We prefer to do this in October because October is in the middle of the semester and can therefore be a dull and trying time for staff. The timing of this event is as important as the sentiment behind it. In the beginning of the semester, there is generally little need for encouragement, and the end of the semester is a time for celebration of what has been done. However, you can do it in any month with an easy change in the name, such as "November Notables" or "April Applause."

Fabulous February

For the majority of the United States and Canada, February—with its overcast skies, cold weather, and lack of holidays and breaks—can seem like one of the longest months of the year, even though it's the shortest. Finding ways to brighten and warm up the mood inside the building can help everyone overcome the winter blahs. We like to make February fabulous by doing something festive on Fridays. Each Friday has a theme such as "Fresh Fruit Friday," "Chili Cook-Off Friday," "Fabulous Fudge Friday," or "Teachers Love Chocolate Friday" (for the Friday closest to Valentine's Day). If money is available, the administration can foot the bill for some or all of the food, or teachers can be asked to bring items. Have someone besides yourself coordinate these events in case you are called away at the last minute or pulled into another event.

In addition to food, having students give Valentine's Day cards to teachers to thank them for their service can be another way to make teachers feel appreciated. Door decorating contests, including themes such as Valentine's Day, Black History Month, or general school spirit, can also be fun breaks in the monotonous school days, and most people love a competition. The brightly covered doors can add a bit of color to the halls as teachers and students wait for spring to arrive. You can create different categories so there is more than one winner. Consider "Best Door" for each grade level, "Most Creative," "Best Use of Materials," and "Most Academic." We recommend having a committee consisting of teachers, staff, and administrators to choose the winners. Winners can then be announced over the intercom and displayed on a bulletin board, TV screen in the lobby, or website. You can also award certificates or mini-trophies.

Faculty Superlatives

We're all familiar with the superlative awards given to graduating high school students in categories such as "most likely to succeed," "best dressed," and "most school spirit." Students appreciate this kind of personal recognition, and we have found that teachers do, too. Establish a variety of categories and have staff members vote for each one. Create certificates for the winners, and hand them out at the end of the year wrap-up. Categories could include:
- Most likely to remember a student's name in 10 years
- Most likely to have been in the principal's office as a student
- Best dressed
- Teacher I would have liked to have had as a teacher
- Best smile

- Most likely to continue teaching even after winning the lottery
- Best sense of humor
- Most creative
- Teacher whose classroom I would most want my own child in

Thank Yous

While this might seem like a simple thing, don't underestimate the power of a simple thank you. If a teacher or team has worked especially hard on a project, take the time to email the whole faculty to acknowledge the effort and thank those involved. Handwritten thank-you notes slipped into a teacher's mailbox can be very meaningful to the recipient as well.

Informal Observation Notes

On a daily basis, you will be in and out of a number of classrooms. Not every visit to a classroom is a formal visit; many are just walk-throughs, or you may simply be in the room to get a student or give the teacher a piece of information. If you notice a teacher do something positive, you can easily take a moment or two to leave a note or send an email complimenting the teacher specifically on what you saw. Notes such as "You are doing a great job" tend to hold little significance to the recipient. But teachers truly appreciate a note that starts with, "When

I was in your classroom today" and then includes a specific comment such as "your grouping of students was highly effective" or "I was very impressed with the activity you were leading and would like for you to share it with your teacher team."

It is important to make notes like this timely, so leave the handwritten note in the teacher's box before the end of the school day. An email can be written on your smartphone as you walk down the hall from the teacher's room or at the latest by the end of the day. Waiting days or weeks tends to have less impact. Both the teacher and the principal are likely to have forgotten the specifics of the visit, making meaningful comments hard to write and the sincerity of the note harder for the teacher to believe.

Create a Culture of Shared Leadership

Perhaps nothing can make teachers feel more valued than being part of the leadership in the school, which is why creating a culture of shared leadership is so important. Shared leadership requires multiple perspectives to make the best decisions possible for students. Shared leadership can look different in different schools, but it is always about finding ways for teachers to be involved in school-based decisions and allowing them to be integral to the design of curriculum, instruction, and assessment in the classroom. Shared leadership allows all staff members to share credit (and responsibility) for the results of the decisions made. Because people support what they help create, sharing leadership often generates greater commitment and dedication of staff members.

General Aspects of Shared Leadership

Here are some important items to remember when creating a culture of shared leadership. First, don't ask for feedback and input on something the school has no control over, such as offerings in the school's cafeteria or the hours of the school day. Asking teachers for feedback on something you can't change will make teachers feel as if their time has been wasted, and if you act as if you will make the change and don't, teachers might feel betrayed.

Second, shared leadership does not mean leadership without vision or no leadership at all. You are the captain of the ship, and while you will seek input from all involved, you have to continue to be the leader of the process so the rest of the crew doesn't try to take the ship off in a direction that was never intended—or worse yet, sink it.

Third, don't discount teachers without giving them a chance. It can be tempting to think that first-year teachers will have nothing of value to add because they lack experience or to think that a particularly grouchy teacher may not be able to give any useful insight, but these preconceived ideas don't allow for true shared leadership. Ignoring these teachers' contributions might mean missing out on some great ideas from an unexpected source. If your fears are proven right, and the new teacher talks more than she listens or the grouchy teacher is continuously negative without offering a solution to any problem, then you can try to mentor them and discuss what changes you would like to see in their behavior. Give them opportunities to observe others taking an appropriate and positive role in shared leadership. If nothing else works, then you can remove them from the leadership role, but at least at that point you will have proof of why the removal needs to happen and not just a gut feeling.

The Leadership Team

One way to create this culture is to have a leadership team. A leadership team is made up of representatives from important groups within the school. You and your administrative team are always one part. The rest of the team is made up of content leaders, grade-level leaders, instructional coaches, or other key people whose opinion you would like to have in the decision-making process. Some leadership teams expand even more and include students, parents, and community or business partners. The topics you choose to have the leadership team address may help determine who you choose to have on it. It should be clear to everyone on the team and everyone affected by its decisions why those particular people were chosen and what issues the team will decide upon.

Leadership teams can be used to make decisions such as how to spend certain funds, what professional development to offer, or how to implement state requirements. When looking specifically at funds, instead of calculating how to divide an amount by teacher or department or student, have the team holistically assess what resources they have and what resources they need. Reviewing test score data is one part of that assessment, but it is not the only source. Schools should look at what skills, supplies, or materials the students will need as they move on to the next level and consider if they are adequately preparing elementary students for middle school or middle school children for high school. Schools should also look at the curriculum as it changes and is developed. Will teachers need things like hands-on science kits or software to support instruction?

Shared leadership flips the focus from what teachers need to effectively teach to what students need to effectively learn. When the student is the center of the discussion, consensus is easier to reach. A leadership team needs to

know how much things cost to run a school. Items to consider include:
- How much do we spend a year on copy machine costs?
- How much do we spend a year on copy paper costs?
- How much do we spend a year on art supplies for art classes?
- How much do we spend a year on musical instruments?
- How much do we spend a year on technology hardware?
- How much do we spend a year on technology software?
- How much would it cost to add an additional teacher with salary and benefits?
- How much would it cost to run a Saturday or afterschool detention?

The more relevant and timely the data and information the principal shares, the more equipped the leadership team is to make a decision.

Finance isn't the only topic for a leadership team. School policy changes should be vetted through shared leadership as well. Since teachers are the closest staff members to students in a school, they are a valuable resource for keeping their figurative finger on the pulse of the student body. They listen and hear what students are talking about. If you are looking for a good incentive for kids, ask teachers. They almost always have low-cost ideas for how to motivate students. In that same vein, they also know what regulations students feel most strongly about.

> ### Stories from the Field
>
> A high school principal questioned the validity of a long-standing school policy that allowed any student with two or fewer absences per semester in a given class to be exempt from the semester exam in that class. The principal worried that students could graduate from his school having never taken a comprehensive examination, which is not sound preparation for college. He met with his leadership team, which included teachers, parents, and students, to discuss the policy. The students liked the policy because it took pressure off them before the holidays and the end of the year. The teachers were glad to have high daily attendance because there was less makeup work for absences. The parents on the team questioned the policy, not because of the academic implications, but because their children were insisting on going to school even when they were very sick. A mother explained that her child with a 103-degree fever came to school, which

> meant she was contagious. Kids coming to school sick created a less healthy environment.
>
> After listening to all these opinions, the principal removed exam exemptions related to attendance—except for seniors. This was a small compromise that did not delete the privilege altogether. However, attendance among students dropped once the incentive for underclassmen was removed.

This story highlights one of the most challenging parts of shared leadership: Everyone has a voice, and sometimes the voices disagree. All sides—the teachers, the students, and the parents—had valid considerations, but when writing, changing, or implementing policies, a principal needs to operate under the philosophy of what is in the best interest for the most kids. The key with shared leadership is to make sure all parties have a voice and feel heard. Generally, people can live with others disagreeing with their perspective if they feel their perspective was fully considered and understood.

Growing Effective Teachers into Effective Teacher Leaders

Principals are highly protective of their talented teachers. They need them because of what they do for kids, for their school's image, and for the high test scores they generate. Secretly principals may think, "If I had 10 teachers like Ms. Lorenzo, I would have the best school in the district." The temptation is to take that teacher and crown her a teacher leader with a special title or stipend or, in extreme cases, even an office. It's a great idea. Except, it doesn't work, at least not for most teachers.

Teachers are cerebral beings by nature. They need to think about ideas, consider alternatives, and develop a creative spin. They cannot be figuratively pushed out of the nest and expected to fly as a teacher leader. They are used to leading children, people smaller and younger with less experience and knowledge. Expecting teachers to transition from teaching kids to leading peers is unreasonable. Leading peers often means leading people you admire and respect, people who may be older or wiser or have more or less talent. It can be an uncomfortable feeling for the teacher.

Provide structure for the effective teacher to evolve into an effective teacher leader. Just as we use training wheels when teaching a child to ride a bike, start small. Ask the teacher to lead an event, one that has a beginning and an end. There could be a science fair or a career night, and this is the opportunity to allow a teacher to begin to spread her leadership wings. The benefit of leading an event is that there is time for reflection at the conclusion of it. This helps the teacher see the bigger task of leadership, if even only for one small part of a day. Providing professional readings about peer coaching in the form of books or journals can also be valuable to help teachers transition from leading students to leading adults.

When developing teacher leaders, principals must be careful not to put teachers in a position that compromises their role as a peer. Teacher leaders are not supervisors, nor are they the school snitch. Teachers don't need more bosses telling them what not to do, they need more ideas for supporting their work as they perfect their craft. In situations where teacher leaders are most effective, the relationship between the teacher leader and peer is mutually beneficial and the continual exchange of ideas and professional banter promotes synergy.

***

Creating an environment where teachers feel welcomed, valued, appreciated, and heard is an important step in the process of leading a school to academic success. Teachers are more likely to put in the extra hours of work necessary to raise student achievement when they feel like that work will be noticed and appreciated. There are perhaps hundreds of other ways that principals recognize their staff. The particular methods used are not as important as the sentiment conveyed. Keep your focus on ensuring that all teachers are recognized for what they bring to the school and are given opportunities to shape the progress of the school.

CHAPTER FIVE

Working with New and Veteran Teachers

The process of supporting and developing talented teachers begins with the first interview and continues on through the speech you give about a teacher when he retires after 30 or more years of service to students. While few principals will work with any particular teacher from the beginning of his career to the end, all principals will have to work with a variety of teachers at various career stages. Knowing how to work with each group is necessary to successfully lead them. This chapter provides guidelines for working with new teachers, young teachers (not necessarily the same as new), and veteran teachers.

Working with New Teachers

With the variety of certification programs designed to bring experienced professionals into the classroom, a new teacher could just as easily be 40 as 22 years old. While their ages may be different, new teachers often share some common characteristics.

- **They lack knowledge.** New teachers usually lack knowledge about how school works on a daily basis. This lack of knowledge will differ greatly depending on the training teachers received prior to starting in the field, but unless they worked in your specific school before, they will have a lack of knowledge about the way things are done there. Even if a teacher student-taught in the building, a full-time teacher has different responsibilities from a student teacher. New teachers sometimes expect your school to be like the one where they went to school, or they expect students to act like they did in school. These expectations can make it more difficult for new teachers to adjust to their job, especially teachers who go to work in an environment that is dramatically different from the one they experienced.
- **They lack experience.** New teachers most likely have not yet been yelled at by a parent, lied to by a student, or pressured by a fellow teacher to disregard the rules. While they may have had a variety of life experiences, they will have many new ones in the classroom and will need help to keep from being blindsided or making the wrong decision when these events occur.

- **They may take on too much.** Often, new teachers think that they will change the world of every student they encounter. They may believe that if they do not have every assignment graded the day after it's turned in—while also creating an amazing lesson that would earn them perfect scores on an evaluation and calling the parent of every child to either praise or discuss concerns every night—then they are in fact a failure as a teacher. This self-imposed pressure can be overwhelming for a new teacher and can be the cause of burnout or emotional or physical distress. New teachers often need a gentle dose of reality to realize that excellence may be something to strive for, but it is not worth driving themselves to exhaustion in pursuit of it. They also need to realize that perfection is not your expectation; rather, you are looking for teachers who are consistently trying to do their best and continuing to grow in their practice.
- **They will not become veterans overnight.** Sometimes new teachers expect to have everything under control and have a complete grasp on the job after a month or semester. Sometimes principals expect this, too. The truth is it can take a year or more before a teacher is able to work with the

efficiency and authority of a veteran, and expecting otherwise from new teachers is not fair.

There is also a different type of new teacher—one who is simply new to the building. These new teachers have experience teaching but lack school-specific knowledge. Sometimes, bad habits and incorrect knowledge gained at another school can be even worse than a simple lack of knowledge. For example, if a teacher is used to turning in paperwork late at one school, she may think that is okay at the next school. A teacher who is regularly absent without being questioned at one school may feel targeted when a principal identifies a disturbing attendance pattern at another school.

A concern of bringing in experienced teachers who are new to your school is that they may not be willing to learn the ways of your school or to change any behaviors that do not work for you. When that happens, these teachers need to be supported similarly to how you support beginning teachers to ensure that the behaviors you want to see are crystal clear. At the same time, respect them for what they do know and don't belittle or patronize them.

High-Quality New Teachers: What to Look For

Hiring good employees can mean a wide variety of things depending on your situation. It is possible that a very good hire for school A is not the best hire for school B because schools have different needs. Teachers are not interchangeable factory workers. Every school has its own spirit, its own core set of driving beliefs, and, just like in families, its own idiosyncrasies that make working there far different from working at the school down the road.

While there is no fool-proof system to choosing a great teacher every single time, there are some tangible and intangible characteristics to look for. Not every effective teacher will have all of these characteristics, so you need to decide which are nonnegotiable for you. For example, liking children is a common nonnegotiable. An English teacher who loves literature is wonderful, but what you want to hear is that the teacher likes children.

Here are some important characteristics to look for when hiring new teachers.

CERTIFICATION AND CONTENT KNOWLEDGE

Teachers with full certification and a major in their field will positively affect how well students do in that area. This is not surprising. The more comfortable and confident teachers are with subject matter, the better able they are to convey that information to students. Teachers who are more comfortable in their content knowledge are more likely to have active classrooms where inquiry is used for a deepening of student knowledge rather than passive classrooms where the curriculum is simplified and worksheets are the most-used curricular tool.

While this can be especially apparent in upper grades, it can also have an effect at the elementary school level. Research has shown that teacher knowledge can have an effect on student performance as early as first grade. Regardless of the age of the students or the subject area, it is important for you to be sure the candidate you're considering is competent and comfortable in the appropriate content and will be able to actively engage students in their learning.

While checking to see if a teacher has proper certifications is a fairly straightforward process, the process of ensuring that a teacher truly understands the subject to be taught is actually more difficult. A person can do the work to pass certain courses without having an in-depth understanding of the subject matter. If you are concerned about the content knowledge of a candidate but don't feel comfortable assessing that knowledge, bring in a valued teacher or academic coach to interview the person. You can also set up a time for them to "talk shop," which will allow your current employee to assess the knowledge and skill level of the candidate. Having candidates describe in writing how they would explain or teach a particular content-specific concept to a student can also be a way to assess content knowledge while also assessing written communication skills.

TEACHER FLEXIBILITY, CREATIVITY, AND ADAPTABILITY

Teachers who are able to change their teaching style and approach as needed tend to be the most successful in the classroom, and their students tend to be more successful on state-mandated tests as well as in life outside of the classroom. This flexibility and adaptability are also necessary in dealing with classroom management and the day-to-day unexpected events that happen in every school (such as assemblies, fire drills, and snow days) that often throw off the best laid plans of any teacher.

Here are some questions to ask that can help you get a feel for a teacher's flexibility and creativity:
- What would you do if 25 percent of your students were not understanding the material?
- What would you do if a lesson you were giving was bombing?

- Tell me about a time when you planned something and things did not go at all as you had planned. What did you do?
- How do you know if your students are learning what they are supposed to know?

TEACHER RESPONSIVENESS

A teacher who is responsive is viewed more positively by students and parents and tends to have better student outcomes than less responsive teachers. Responsive teachers are actively involved in the learning of the classroom and can move between leading, facilitating, and participating in classroom discussion. They tend to ask more questions than they answer, helping lead students to the correct answers rather than feeding the answers to them. They encourage students to think for themselves, have a variety of instructional strategies in their toolbox, and are willing to change plans in the moment.

While there is no clear way to see responsiveness in an interview, you can ask questions about a typical day in the teacher's classroom or what the teacher would do in a variety of classroom situations to get an idea of responsiveness. Those questions could include ones like the following:

- What would you do if students asked you a question you think they should be able to figure out on their own?

- How do you train students to think independently?
- What are ways that you encourage active participation in learning in your classroom?

TEACHER USE OF DATA

The more teachers understand and use data, the better their students tend to perform.

Data is about more than just test scores. It is not enough for teachers to be able to share how well their students did on the final assessment. An effective teacher needs to have a variety of ways of collecting different types of data—including formative, summative, individual, and group—on a continuous basis as well as ideas and plans for what to do with that data. Don't judge teachers' understanding of data based on whether they can explain the difference between the mean and the mode or explain what standard deviation is. Rather, evaluate whether they understand what the data is saying about student performance and in turn about their own instruction, and if they can speak in concrete ways about how data has changed or will change their plans in the classroom.

Teachers should go through a regular reflection process in which they make decisions about student needs based on the data. For example, teachers should be able to tell which students need extra help on a skill or performance indicator based on how the student has performed on multiple assessments. We want teachers to be able to diagnose problems and make adjustments before it's too late.

When interviewing first-year teachers, you can ask about data use during student teaching, if appropriate, or about data use in another job or experience. If an interviewee has no particular experience with data use, you can create a scenario based on real data from your school and ask what the candidate would do with it.

TEACHER DEDICATION

Teachers who are dedicated to improving the performance of their students as well as to the overall vision of the school are more effective than those who are not. Teaching can be a very demanding job, and sometimes it is only that dedication that carries teachers through trying times. Teaching is not a job one gets into for the paycheck or the vacations, and you will want to be on the lookout for teachers who may be in it for those reasons.

Dedication is something that should be evident in the work and answers of an interviewee. You might look for dedication in how an interviewee describes his part in a project or the work he did in another school or another job. You might also see dedication in volunteer projects that the interviewee has been involved with. Doing extra unpaid work often shows the dedication of a person, but remember that just because a candidate doesn't volunteer on a regular basis doesn't mean that person won't be dedicated to the job.

TEACHER BELIEFS AND PHILOSOPHIES

Beliefs refer to what a person thinks is true or should be true. "All children can learn" is a belief. **Philosophies** are guiding principles that govern all behavior. "We do not use negative signage in our school" is a philosophy.

When interviewing a candidate, try to discern whether the person's beliefs and philosophies fit in with yours—and therefore the school's. Otherwise effective teachers may feel unsupported or dissatisfied at the school, and thus less effective, if they disagree with or do not understand your philosophies and beliefs. You may find it hard to fully trust or fully support a teacher whose philosophies and beliefs differ greatly from yours.

To get an idea of a candidate's beliefs and philosophies, you can ask a straightforward question like, "What is your teaching philosophy?" or "What are your beliefs about teaching?" Either of these questions will likely elicit the information you're looking for. Be aware that this is a question that most interviewees expect and are prepared to answer, and one that they have probably been crafting since their first education class in college. You are likely to get a polished answer, but what you're looking for are sincerity and alignment with your own philosophies and beliefs.

A teacher's well-crafted response may simply be something she thinks you want to hear rather than what she actually thinks. Regardless of whether you ask directly about philosophies and beliefs, it can be helpful to look for evidence of them in candidates' answers to other questions related to how they would interact with different types of students and respond in different situations.

TEACHER-STUDENT RELATIONSHIPS

While all teachers don't need to have a sunny disposition and talk incessantly about their love of children, it is important that teachers see the importance of building relationships with students and see teaching as something that is done *with* students and not *to* them. It is also important that teachers see students as teachable. You might not expect someone who doesn't believe these things to apply for a teaching job, but it happens, and this type of person can slip through the interview process if you assume otherwise.

As you interview, listen for how candidates refer to students and describe the teaching and learning process. Listen for responses that are student-centered and active. For example, it is interesting to ask how candidates teach a student who dislikes the content they are teaching. Does the teacher describe trying to connect the subject matter to something the student is interested in or providing some real-world, authentic application? Such answers are far preferable to answers that indicate the teacher simply believes that not everyone likes all content and sometimes they just have to sit there and be quiet. Asking what was most memorable from a previous teaching experience or what the teacher thinks of a particular difficult student (either real or imagined) may also clue you into how the interviewee feels about students.

Interview Questions to Ask

Interviewing candidates is a skill that needs to be honed, and in time you will develop your own questions and learn for yourself what you're looking for in candidates. While effective interview questions are helpful, you need to determine in your own mind what the "right" answers are and what you are listening for. Have an idea of what you're hoping to hear when you ask questions.

Here are some questions we like to ask and the types of answers we typically look for.

"Walk me through a typical day in your classroom." While the answer will vary depending on if it is being answered by a Spanish teacher or a computer teacher—or a third-grade teacher or a tenth-grade teacher—there are universals to listen for, including:
- The teacher starts with an introductory activity and has the students engaged in learning the moment they enter the room.

- The teacher changes activities on a frequent basis that is appropriate for the age group.
- Students are doing more work than the teacher.
- There is a plan to differentiate to meet the wide range of abilities in the class.
- There is a level of innovation. (Remember, this is a job interview, and if the teacher can't think of something very interesting to describe in an interview, it could be because the teacher does not value having "a hook" to engage students' interests.)
- Students have opportunities to practice new skills.
- There is a built-in plan for the teacher to assess student learning.

Of course, a teacher could give several other valuable comments, which is why it is so important for you to know what you are listening for.

"What are you looking for in a principal?" This triggers some essential beliefs about how the candidate expects to be treated as an employee and helps illuminate whether the match between supervisor and subordinate will work. The most common response for this answer is "support." It's no surprise that teachers want support from their principals. When teachers give that response, many of them will pause and then tell a story about a time they received tremendous support from a principal—or a time they felt let down by one. It is poor interview strategy to criticize a former supervisor, but many candidates make that error, particularly when they are caught off guard with a question they were not expecting to answer.

While it is valuable to know that a candidate will speak critically of a former principal, it is almost even more telling when the opposite occurs. It is beneficial to hear teachers describe a time they felt supported because it tells if their past experience will align with what you are in the habit of providing. For example, a teacher could indicate that the principal taught her class for her when she had to leave early one day. If you would not do that in your school, it might indicate a large chasm between what the candidate expects and what you are willing or able to provide. Knowing what people consider as "supportive" speaks volumes about not only what experience they have, but also in what ways they will be needy.

The best answer to this question is not "support." Rather, when candidates indicate that they are looking for a principal who will help them grow, be a better teacher, or improve, that shows that they are committed to lifelong learning for themselves as individuals. They see their supervisor's role as far more broad than merely protecting them from the shouting of an irate parent.

> ## Stories from the Field
>
> In a job interview, a teacher described her former principal as being a great principal. When the interviewer asked for a story to describe what was great about the former principal, the candidate talked about how he mowed the school's grass on the weekends and painted the bleachers of the football stadium himself one summer. The teacher described these activities as showing how deep the principal's commitment to the school was.

The answer that teacher gave shows that her former principal was committed to doing work for the school with his own hands and on his own time. However, the interviewer needs to consider if that is consistent with what he believes is a great principal. One could easily argue that principals who do the manual labor themselves can't be great principals because they are allowing issues that someone else could take care of to monopolize their time. Alternatively, one could argue that a great principal cares about every detail in the school including lawn care. The "right" answer is in the eye of the beholder. If you do not do any of the maintenance work, will this candidate think that you are not effective and thereby be unsatisfied working under you?

"What do you know about our school?" If candidates have had three hours' notice or more in advance of a job interview, they have had time to at least peruse the school's website, find out superficial information like the mascot, memorize a few "buzz words," and review the vision and beliefs. Googling the school principal's name will often pull up some press clippings about the school and its recent good—or bad—news. Candidates who take the time to look, search, and learn are going to take those innate characteristics into the classroom, and that inquisitive spirit inspires learning. Candidates who respond to the question with "not much" or give an excuse about why they did not have time to learn about the school are showing an example of the effort they give to tasks.

Here are a few other questions you might ask, along with thoughts about what to listen for in a good answer.

- You have asked a student to stop blurting out in class (or another typical student misbehavior) and the student stops, but then quickly begins the behavior again. What do you do? **Listen for:** Consistent rules and consequences, description of undesired behavior as opposed to undesirable child, partnering with parents, no group punishments.
- If you have given a formative assessment and 50 percent of the students have not done

well, what would you do? What if it were 25 percent? What about 80? **Listen for:** Reteaching for those who need it, analysis of assessment, and reassessing after reteaching.
- A student has shown over weeks that she does not understand the material. What do you do? **Listen for:** Reteaching in a different manner followed by reassessing. Providing extra support for any learner who needs it.
- A student who has been continuously behind in class has now come to you toward the end of the grading period to ask for help and makeup work. What do you do? **Listen for:** How the teacher would have intervened during the grading period to prevent this from happening, assessing whether the student knows some of the material so remaining work can be prioritized. Willingness to work with students.
- So much of teaching today is about managing data, such as attendance, grades, behavior, and more. How do you handle all of these various demands on your time while still creating effective lessons for students? **Listen for:** Procedures that make the management duties blend in on a routine basis.
- What is an acceptable failure rate? **Listen for:** A determination to reteach and reassess after student failure as opposed to citing an

arbitrary number as an acceptable failure rate. Assumption of responsibility for the work that needs to be done by the teacher to support the student.

In job interviews, candidates will usually tell you exactly who they are—if you are wise enough to listen.

Other Things to Look For

While these things are not directly related to teaching, they can tell you a lot about a candidate.

CLOTHING

Clothing says something about the person wearing it, and interviewees should show up dressed better than you would expect them to be on a daily basis. Dress pants or a skirt and dress shirt are a bare minimum, and a business suit is preferred. If candidates do not take the time to dress professionally for an interview with their future boss, there is no telling how they might show up a few weeks into school or toward the end of the first semester when everyone is struggling to get up and out of bed.

Evaluating a candidate's clothing is not about how fashionable or high-quality the clothes are, but rather about how appropriate the clothing is for the profession of teaching. Some new teachers don't properly judge what is appropriate to wear to school. Maybe an aspiring new teacher shows up at an interview wearing a low-cut tank top. Maybe a young candidate arrives wearing a baseball cap and sneakers. What is fashionable in society or appropriate in another line of work is not necessarily appropriate for a role model to wear in front of young impressionable minds. Dress in an interview might not be a deal breaker, but it needs to be taken into consideration and addressed quickly if there are causes for concern.

Some quick and easy guidelines include:
- Clothing should be age appropriate. You don't want students and teachers dressing the same.
- Teacher clothing should exceed the standards for student clothing. Hence, if students cannot wear torn pants, teachers cannot not wear torn pants.
- Teacher clothing can be appropriate to the job and professional. PE teachers do not need to dress in an oversize T-shirt and sweatpants to be able to work in the gym. They can be comfortably but professionally dressed while leading physical activity.

PROPER GRAMMAR AND COMMUNICATION SKILLS

Teaching is communicating, and in an interview you can assess how the candidate will communicate with students, parents, and other professionals. Clear language that is grammatically correct exudes competence. While every teacher being hired is not an English teacher, all have to communicate both orally and in writing with a wide variety of audiences.

If you have a hard time understanding what a candidate is saying due to improper grammar or a general poor ability to communicate, then it is probably safe to assume that students and parents will have a problem as well. The candidate's résumé and cover letter are good places to review the candidate's communication skills, but asking candidates to submit a writing sample (as described on "Certification and Content Knowledge") can reveal even more information.

GUT REACTION

Principals deal with many people day after day, and many develop a refined gut instinct about people. Follow that instinct. Many things go on in an interview, and if you have a knee-jerk reaction about a candidate, it is meaningful even if you cannot put your finger on what you're reacting to. If something about the teacher makes you feel uncomfortable, you might want to bring the teacher back for another interview that includes others, such as an assistant principal or content or grade-level team leader. Getting another's perspective on the potential hire might be just what you need to either confirm or calm your uneasy feelings.

There may also be times when you feel that a candidate who is not the strongest on paper is the exact right person for the job. Again, trust your instincts. At its core, interviewing is about one human's response to and assessment of another human, and instinct has a role to play in such interactions. It doesn't mean just getting a feeling and going it with, but rather taking those feelings into account with all other data gained from the interview.

The Effects of New Teachers on Staff Culture

When new teachers join a staff, there is always a risk of cliques or schisms developing. You can help prevent that and preserve a feeling of wholeness by constantly working to maintain a culture where all teachers are valued (see Chapter 4). You can also achieve this by keeping a balance on the leadership team of qualified new teachers and current teachers who have valuable institutional knowledge about the school. (See section entitled "The Leadership Team".) Simple things such as dismissal practices, assemblies, and parent night can prove troublesome if you don't have teachers on the leadership team who can provide knowledge about how things have been done in the past and make observations of what worked well and what needs to be changed. New teachers who come from other schools can provide a fresh perspective and insight into how other schools handle some of these events, too.

You will also need to make sure that new teachers don't flock only to each other and that veteran teachers don't do the same. One way to do this is with a strong mentor program, as described in section entitled "DEVELOP A MENTORSHIP PROGRAM". Another is the faculty social functions created by the morale or sunshine committee, which should include both new and veteran teachers. All of these activities will help create a culture where both groups feel included. You also help propagate this inclusive culture by developing productive working relationships not only with the people you hire, but with everyone on staff.

Supporting New Teachers

Once the new batch of teachers has been hired, the arduous task of helping them make it through their first year begins. You can do many things to make the first year less daunting to new teachers and more successful for all involved.

ONBOARDING

The onboarding process is for new teachers to learn the particular ways things are done at the school. The participation of brand new teachers and teachers new to the building is of equal importance. The onboarding process can contain several aspects, but these are the most typical.

- **Meetings with the assigned mentors.** (See section entitled "DEVELOP A MENTORSHIP PROGRAM" for more on mentors.) At these initial mentor meetings, the new teachers and their mentors should discuss procedures for requesting materials, signing in, handling parent complaints, accessing the building on the weekends, getting reimbursed for purchases, and so on.
- **Meetings with other key people.** This can include team or content leads, members of the leadership team, and other key members of the school who may be unofficial leaders. It may also include staff who you have assigned the job of being the "go-to person" for questions (see section entitled "CREATE A CULTURE OF "ASK FIRST""). Veterans you invite to these onboarding events shows the new teachers who you value and who they should look to as role models.
- **Discussions of beliefs and philosophies.** It's important that new teachers understand the beliefs and philosophies that guide the decision-making process at your school. It's not enough to know what we do, we want teachers to know why we do it as well.
- **Distribution of relevant vocabulary.** This includes special names for advisory groups, weekly newsletters, and important acronyms.

Giving teachers a list of these with definitions can be helpful.

- **Distribution of information about programs.** If your school is involved in reform efforts or other initiatives, new teachers will need basic information about them. These programs tend to come with their own vocabulary and acronyms, too, so covering general vocabulary with these is also a good idea.
- **Discussion of important procedures.** Make sure new teachers know how the school handles evaluations, time off, guest speakers, media usage, and so on.
- **Review of a "Frequently Asked Questions" list.** The list should cover issues that often come up as well as the name and contact information of a designated "Ask First" person. (See section entitled "CREATE A CULTURE OF "ASK FIRST"".)
- **Tour of the school.** Include each new teacher's classroom, resource rooms, book rooms (location of the text books), where to get copy paper, and so on.
- **Distribution of important school-provided materials.** This might include keys, textbooks, ID, and more.
- **Set-up time.** Teachers set up their classrooms.

Another aspect of onboarding that can sometimes be overlooked is the process of making new teachers feel as if they are a part of the school community. This can be done in a variety of ways and should be representative of the school community. For example, many schools have lanyards that all of their faculty members wear on a daily basis. Having a ceremony where the new teachers first get their lanyards and are officially welcomed to the school team can be a way to make new teachers feel included. Also, see Chapter 4 for a more thorough discussion of making staff feel welcomed and valued.

The time for onboarding can be in the summer before school starts, during in-service time at the beginning of the school year, or after school at the beginning of the year. You might also continue with onboarding events throughout the year as needed.

DEVELOP A MENTORSHIP PROGRAM

Creating a mentor program accomplishes a variety of goals at once and has been proven to help teachers perform better. Teachers who are mentored tend to have a reduced chance of burnout and improved classroom management and lesson development.

Not only do the new teachers and their students benefit, but the mentors and the school climate benefit as well. Mentor teachers get a chance to work on their leadership skills, and for those who would like to move into administrative or other types of leadership roles later in their career, this can be a good stepping stone. Building bonds between new and veteran teachers can help the school community function as one. The overall school climate can benefit because it encourages all teachers to keep their classrooms and minds open to the ideas of others.

When you choose mentors, don't simply choose people on the same hall together or who teach the same subject or grade level. Choosing mentors will make a statement about who you think is doing a quality job and is the right person to direct a new teacher. If you are new, try to get as much feedback about potential mentors from the previous principal as possible before assigning them. Over the years, you may want to keep track of who you have chosen to be a mentor, who has done well as a mentor, and—of those not chosen—who could potentially do well.

Once you have chosen those teachers who would make acceptable mentors, the process of assigning mentors can begin. Keep proximity, grade and subject, personality types, and similar life experiences in mind. Try to connect people based on what you know about all of those involved. While you will most likely not know new hires very well, you will have an idea from interviews and résumés. Examples of potential pairings might include teachers who have moved from middle school to high school or middle school to elementary school, or teachers who both started teaching later in life.

We recommend that newly hired teachers who have experience elsewhere also get mentors, though you need to select their mentors carefully. Most veteran teachers are not likely to benefit from a second-year teacher as a mentor. Instead, choose one of the most veteran teachers or else choose a teacher who made the transition from one school to another with great success.

Don't try to force relationships that aren't working or end relationships that are. Because you will not know the intricacies of new teachers' personalities and, if you are new, the intricacies of mentors' personalities either, sometimes the best planned matches will not work or unexpected matches will form. That is okay as long as you can adjust and new teachers get support from veterans you value as mentors.

The actual design of the mentor program can vary greatly depending on the school, size of the teaching population, and the ratio of new teachers to returning teachers, but regardless of the look, a successful program will have similar attributes. It will provide opportunities in and out of the school day for mentors and new teachers to spend time together, and these opportunities will not only exist at the beginning of the school year, but will continue throughout the first year and possibly into the second.

Provide mentors with a list of areas to continually monitor with their partners, including classroom management, lesson planning, assessments, academic success of students on those assessments, plans based on the results of those assessments, grading, paperwork, relationships with students, parents, teachers, staff, and administration, and the new teacher's overall health and well-being. New teachers should also be encouraged to come to each meeting with any questions or concerns. Mentors and their partners will share a variety of forms of communication, including emails, phone calls, classroom visits, and face-to-face conversations.

In addition to gathering feedback about how each mentor relationship is going, solicit feedback throughout the year from everyone involved as to the program's successes and failures so you can make improvements every year. Soliciting feedback and making changes as needed should always be a part of any program implementation.

CREATE A CULTURE OF "ASK FIRST"

It is far better for new teachers to ask questions than it is for them to push blindly ahead and make mistakes that can cause problems at school. If teachers are not encouraged to ask questions without fear, the school will not run as well as it possibly could. Make a list of people who new teachers can ask about different topics, or designate one person to be the go-to person for all questions. These questions might include everything from "Where do I park?" to "When is payday?"

The go-to person should not be you, because you most likely do not have the time to devote adequate support to all new teachers, and a new teacher may be reluctant to "bother" you with questions. In addition, developing a variety of trusted relationships helps increase teacher retention.

Don't make your go-to person a formal mentor to a teacher, but rather a person who can provide basic correct information to all teachers in a timely manner. Make sure the person you designate understands that she will likely answer the same questions a dozen or more times every school year. She will need to be patient as well as responsive, because teachers can't wait weeks for answers to their questions. It's a good idea to have this person create the list of frequently asked questions as a part of the onboarding process (see section entitled "DEVELOP A MENTORSHIP PROGRAM").

SUPPORT IN THE CLASSROOM

Often, the most difficult aspect of teaching for brand new teachers is classroom management. You and your administrative team need to be frequent visitors in the classrooms of new teachers to support them. Visiting frequently will also prevent you from being blindsided by issues in the classroom. As soon as you notice or suspect problems, take steps to support the teacher. This support can come from you, an assistant principal, a mentor, or a specially assigned person with particular strength in working with teachers on classroom management. Some districts might offer such people, but we recommend filling it with a respected veteran within the building.

Teachers who are new to the building but not to teaching need to be checked on frequently, as well, to ensure their transition to the new building is going well and their style of teaching works within the focus of the school. For example, a teacher who raises his voice regularly may not fit within the patterns that have been established for appropriate adult behavior. This teacher will need support and retraining to learn a different style of addressing students.

CONTINUOUS SUPPORT

Support for brand new or new-to-the-building teachers should not end after the first week of school. Continue to put extra effort into helping them throughout the school year, and for many new teachers, you may want to continue into the second year as well. Continuous support and training lead to stronger teachers. Ensure that mentors check in with new teachers throughout the year.

When events occur throughout the year, make sure to send extra information to new teachers about what will be happening and what the expectations are. As with students, don't hold teachers accountable for things that have never been explained to them or for which expectations have never been shared. It is also a good idea to get feedback from new teachers about specific parts of your support for them to see what worked and what did not in order to improve for the next year.

Working with Young Teachers

Young teachers can bring vitality and enthusiasm to your faculty. Often, they have the latest research-based instructional strategies and energy that will have them charging out of the gate on the first day of school. You may need to help them pace themselves by discouraging them from taking on too much, but for the most part you will do well to encourage that energy and channel it in positive ways.

You'll also want to watch out for potential risks when working with young teachers. Because of their limited professional experience, they may not always understand what is professionally appropriate, and they may not always appreciate the seriousness and weight of the job of teacher. Being a teacher is not the same as being a waitress or even being a banker. The public has higher expectations for teachers. For example, a DUI for a banker wouldn't be a blip on the public's radar, while a DUI for a teacher can be breaking news.

The following guidelines are important for all teachers, but the risks more commonly come up with young teachers.

Social Media

Many teachers are active on social media these days, but young teachers can be especially active—and vulnerable to making social media mistakes that can be costly to their reputation and career. Be upfront with your teachers that they need to be conservative in using social media in their personal lives. Obviously teachers have lives outside of school, and they may use social media to stay in touch with their friends and families, but teachers need to be careful not to post images or text that might reflect poorly on them or the school. In some communities, it is considered unprofessional for a teacher to post a photo of himself at a nightclub. Similarly, while teachers are entitled to their political beliefs, they must keep in mind that not everyone will agree with them, and things they post on a social media site can interfere with their ability to communicate with the parents of the students they serve.

For these reasons, mixing social media for social purposes and teacher purposes is ill-advised. If teachers have personal Facebook, Twitter, Instagram, or other accounts, advise them to use tight privacy settings preventing students and families from accessing them.

At the same time, social media can be a great way to connect with students and take learning in new directions. It can also be a convenient and effective way to stay in touch with students and families. Just be sure to keep personal and professional accounts totally separate. An online discussion about the symbolism of blood in *Macbeth* does not belong alongside a teacher's pictures from her 23rd birthday party. There are plenty of sites that are specifically for education that tech-savvy teachers can use to actively engage students without using their personal social media accounts.

A lot can be said for keeping our worlds separate to ensure our own privacy.

Stories from the Field

A young, first-year teacher had a blog on which he talked about students and the school where he worked, and the majority of what he wrote was negative in nature. It was a way for him to electronically "vent" about a stressful day or situation. While the teacher did not mention the name of the school, anyone who knew him knew where he worked, and it would have been fairly easy for anyone, such as a local media outlet, to figure it out.

Teachers writing about their school and students on blogs, Facebook, Twitter, or other social media is now a common practice, and schools can be held accountable for these public comments. Also, employees can find themselves in trouble for inappropriate comments. What used to be water cooler or—in the education world—copy machine talk, is now exposed to the wider world, and that comes with ramifications.

Tell teachers: Unless you are comfortable with it being on the front page of the local newspaper or being read by your principal, don't put it on social media. Once something is out there, it is out there, and it is not going away. Depending on privacy settings, it can be seen by anyone at any time.

If you see or learn of something inappropriate on an employee's social media that is specifically about the school, address it right away because it can affect the school's reputation. Request that the employee remove it immediately, but make this request with a witness present. It is possible that the employee may say that you are trying to infringe on her First Amendment rights, so following the district's policy, if it exists, is important. If there is no policy, then you will want to talk with your supervisors and get their thoughts on the matter before addressing the situation to ensure that the district will support your plan of action. Remind teachers, too, that principals can and will take what they write in social media into consideration when making decisions about their continued employment or continuation in a particular role in the school.

Clothing

Young teachers sometimes lack teacher-appropriate clothing. Many do not have the budget to buy lots of brand new clothes, and of course you cannot expect them to do so. But you will want to address what is and is not appropriate in a frank manner at the beginning of their employment and at the beginning of every school year. This is especially important at the high school level, where it is possible that only four years separate your youngest teachers from your oldest students.

Some principals do not feel comfortable giving fashion advice, especially males giving advice to female teachers. But you can share some general rules:

- If you are unsure, don't wear it. If you question it in your own head, then it is most likely that someone else will find it inappropriate. Why take the chance?
- At the shortest, skirts should be well below the fingertips when arms are outstretched down by your side.
- Consider dressing older than your age for work. Taking command in the classroom can be hard for young teachers, especially if they

look particularly young or dress in a fashion that is more closely related to their students than their peers. Dressing older can help make this separation easier and can help with classroom management.
- How well can you move in the outfit? Teaching is not a stationary activity, so teachers need to make sure they can move comfortably all day no matter the activity, such as squatting beside a student desk or reaching and bending for student work.

You can even use visuals to show rather than tell teachers about clothing choices. Paper dolls dressed professionally for both men and women can be a lighthearted way to address the situation. If a teacher has a particular problem with dress after the school year starts, you will need to address this individually so the problem does not continue. When addressing clothing, it is often prudent to have another person in the room as a witness; we highly recommend this if the teacher is of the opposite sex from you.

Professional Interactions and Communication

As with social media and clothing, sometimes young teachers push the boundaries of acceptable professional interactions. As always, you are best served to clearly set expectations about behavior early.

Discuss with teachers how they are expected to interact and communicate with students, parents, faculty, staff, and administration. They must remember that parents and students are their "customers," and their interactions need to be professional in nature. That means using proper grammar and common communication guidelines, avoiding slang and acronyms, and refraining from making judgmental statements about students or parents.

As relationships develop, sometimes professional lines can become blurred for teachers, and they may begin to see parents or students as friends. This is a slippery slope and can lead to poor decisions. For example, while a teacher might complain to a friend about how annoying a fellow teacher is, doing this with a parent or student is unacceptable.

One common problem is teachers engaging in the rumor mill—about students, fellow teachers, or events in the school or district. Address the spreading of rumors up front with all teachers, perhaps in a faculty meeting, and keep a watchful eye out for this behavior in all teachers, especially young ones. It is easier to break a habit in a young teacher than change it in a veteran. Make it clear that discussions about students and their behavior or frustrations about other teachers or administration should never take place in front of students.

It can be effective to talk with teachers about real-life examples of appropriate and inappropriate communications that you have seen over the years as a way to show what you expect.

Student-Teacher Separation

As with teacher dress, problems with teacher-student separation come up most commonly at the high school level. Since there can be as few as four years of difference between the oldest students in the building and the youngest teachers, some young teachers may find that they have more in common with students than they do with veteran teachers who are the age of their parents. They are more likely to share common musical tastes, clothing preferences, and favorite movies with students than they are with fellow teachers, especially if there are not many young teachers in the building. It is of vital importance that you and the teacher leaders in the building model proper student-teacher separation and can articulate what that looks like.

What's considered appropriate behavior with students continues to change and become more conservative. Whereas a hug from a male teacher to a female student might have gone unnoticed in years past, it can now be cause for suspension no matter how innocent the intent. Teachers typically get into teaching because they care about kids, and so they often get emotionally involved in their students' lives—that can happen no matter the grade level of the school. It is easy for any teacher, but especially a young or inexperienced one, to get too involved without realizing it. Make sure to clearly express the school's policy on driving students home, spending time with students outside of school, engaging in social media with students, and other aspects relating to student-teacher relationships. Even the most slightly questionable relationships between teachers and students can end up in the media and quickly and easily be blown out of proportion, ruining teachers' careers.

As a guideline for young teachers, advise them to ask themselves if what they are doing with a student could be misconstrued in any way by the media or anyone else. If it could, then they should avoid putting themselves in that position. Physical contact with students and time spent alone or in nonschool-related activities are almost always bad ideas.

While it is critical to share policies about relationships, just as important, if not more so, is sharing policies on what to do if teachers are made privy to very personal information from students, including abuse, suicidal thoughts, bullying, or drug use (either by the student or the parents). Be absolutely sure that district and school policies are clearly laid out and easy to understand. Protecting students from harm, from themselves or from others, is an important and serious part of a teacher's responsibility, but not one that is often covered in a typical education class, so the school must make it a priority to train all teachers on best practices and on their legal and moral responsibilities.

Working with Veteran Teachers

Veteran teachers tend to be a bit more resistant to change than their inexperienced counterparts, but they also tend to get less worked up when new things are thrown their way. Veterans can be your greatest source of help if you treat them with respect and use their positive traits to your advantage.

Been There Done That

Veteran teachers typically have seen many educational reforms come and go, and this experience can be both a benefit and a problem for a new principal—or any principal—trying to enact a change or new program in a school. The benefit can be that veteran teachers tend to take new reforms in stride without panic. They have the mindset that they were here when the last reform came and went, and they will be here when this one comes and goes as well.

That mindset can also be the problem. While this calm can help quiet the fears of new teachers, the idea that the reform will come and go like the others before it can often lead to poor implementation. You need to clearly share the importance of the reform to you and the benefit to students in order to get buy-in from veteran teachers. Acknowledge when a new reform is similar to something done in the past. Share documentation that shows why the reform is needed and how it can help teachers do their jobs better. If you are unable to provide this information, it is highly possible that skeptical veteran teachers are correct to be skeptical, and you may want to rethink the prudence of enacting the change or new reform.

Make Them Feel a Part of the Process

Veteran teachers want to be valued for their experience and their institutional knowledge, and showing that you value them can help move them to your side. The choosing of mentors is a clear way to do that. (See section entitled "DEVELOP A MENTORSHIP PROGRAM".) Asking a veteran teacher to be the go-to person for certain questions can be another way. Make veteran teachers active members of the leadership team and seek their input when planning events or changes. When you do not have a strong need or desire to change the status quo, go along with what the veterans have done. This makes them feel valued and keeps you from reinventing wheels when those you have are still rolling along just fine.

Veteran teachers tend to be more comfortable in their own skin than new teachers, and this generally means that they need less reassurance from others that they are doing a good job or are on the right track. But they should not be forgotten. If veteran teachers see that new teachers get all of the focus and praise while the veterans are consistently overlooked, it can cause a divide between the two groups. To keep this from happening, make sure all committees, leadership teams, and other groups are a good mix of the two. Use veterans to present to the faculty whenever appropriate, showing that they are valued for what they bring to the team. A veteran teacher presenting a new teacher initiative to the entire faculty can also give the initiative credibility. When doing morale or culture cultivating activities, remember to include and recognize both groups of teachers.

The teaching profession is a rewarding road, and those who choose to drive down it do so with the best of intentions. It is your role as the principal to help them navigate their careers from the first mile to the last so they aren't waylaid by potholes or accidents. Remember to teach the behaviors you expect to see and be forthright and timely in addressing problems so teachers have the chance to improve.

***

Hiring and mentoring teachers are arguably the most important jobs a principal does, so they should not be taken lightly. Be intentional in your planning, from preparing to ask the first interview question of your first teacher candidate to choosing veteran teachers to serve on the leadership team. This intentionality will improve the overall quality of your teaching staff and therefore the overall academic success of your students.

CHAPTER SIX

Supporting Teachers at Every Level

Regardless of years of experience, not all teachers perform at the same level. Some stand out as rock stars even in their first few weeks of teaching and really shine by year four or five, while some, even after years of training and mentoring, never make it beyond a basic level of competence. Some teachers start out as middle-of-the-pack performers, or even a little further behind, but because they are responsive to training and willing to learn from experience, they rise from mediocrity to become indispensable standout teachers.

We call these standout teachers "high fliers." Their competence, actions, and ability to adapt help improve student learning and school culture.

Stories from the Field

A first-year teacher, who had always been a high flier in life, came to a school through a nontraditional teaching program, meaning that the teacher had not had sufficient teacher training and had no student teaching experience. She

taught science, an area that was hard to fill, and the school had limited options for hiring. The teacher had a great enthusiasm for teaching and for her subject, so she was brought on board and given the typical support from the school, including regular meetings with a mentor, a content team, a grade-level team, and an assistant principal.

The first year was rough for this teacher. On any given day, she had more students out in the hall than in the classroom, and often the classroom seemed like complete chaos, but the teacher continued to try. The principal saw potential in her and kept her despite the struggles because she was bright, capable, and willing to learn. The teacher learned that classroom management was an area where she needed a lot of help, so she went to trainings and accepted mentoring from other experienced teachers and the principal. Gradually her classroom management improved. Students were engaged in learning rather than being involved in inappropriate behavior or being out of the room. The teacher's test scores went up. This once faltering teacher became a high flier helping to support and train others.

In this example, a teacher appeared underqualified and unpromising, but when taking her personality into consideration along with her willingness to learn and change, the principal discovered that she was actually just a high flier who was in over her head. Patience along with support from the school paid off in the end. This example serves as a reminder that it takes time for some teachers to reach their full potential and that you have to work with teachers where they are to get them where they need to go.

This chapter describes how to identify three types of teachers—"high fliers," "mid fliers," and "low fliers"—as well as how to help each type thrive, grow, or go.

High Fliers

High fliers are those teachers who are impressive to all who work with them or watch them teach. They may come to the school already flying high, or they may need help and support to move up to high-flier status. High fliers generally have above-average intelligence, a high level of dedication to their work and their students, and a willingness to learn and grow. You can recognize high fliers in the classroom by their students' high level of engagement, the quality lessons they are constantly refining, and the positive comfortable atmosphere. High fliers also tend to take on leadership roles and wish to be actively involved in the improvement of the school as a whole. High fliers are not content to just perform at the same level, even if it is a high level. They always see room for improvement and growth and want to be the best at everything they try.

They also tend to flock together regardless of age or years of experience, surrounding themselves with other high fliers. Because of that, high fliers tend to think that everyone else is trying just as hard as they are or performing just as well. While they may know that the quality of their work is high, they often do not realize how much they stand out from others. However, a high flier who becomes content may begin to fall and move into the level of the mid or even low fliers.

How to Communicate with High Fliers

High fliers value straightforward communication and the chance to share their ideas with those who make decisions. They want to be involved in the process of solving problems and are far more likely to fully support any change or required work if they have been involved in the process or have had the importance explained to them. These teachers often benefit from hearing the *why* of a decision or the background information, so it is smart to engage them on important policy changes and initiatives because they will be a much greater help to you if they're informed and on board.

While high fliers like to have thorough communication, they also do not want to have their time wasted, so be clear and concise when communicating with them. In group discussions with high fliers, keep things moving and do not allow the group to digress too far away from the point. High fliers often talk a lot, so you have to be able to move them along in a respectful but time efficient manner.

How to Get High Fliers to Do What Is Needed

High fliers generally will do what is asked and do it better than expected if they find it of value. On the other hand, if they do not see the value, they will do what is required but nothing more.

> ### Stories from the Field
>
> **An administration required that teachers turn in lesson plans on a weekly basis. A high-flying teacher did what was asked and spent time making sure that his lesson plans were detailed and easily understandable to his supervising principal. After weeks of not receiving any feedback or seeing the principal in the classroom, the high flier started submitting the same lesson plans week**

> after week with no changes so that his time could be better spent preparing for student learning rather than documenting it. When this went unnoticed, the high flier realized that the principal was not even looking at the lesson plans and stopped sending them altogether.
>
> Weeks later, in a meeting, the principal praised the high flier and the rest of his department for getting their lesson plans in on time. After the meeting, the teachers talked and admitted that none of them had turned in lesson plans in weeks. The teachers lost respect for the principal and began to question other policies that seemed to be in place for no particular reason.

Even the best teachers tend to underperform or not perform when they see that what they are being asked to do is a waste of time, is not being monitored, or has no positive impact on student achievement. To get high fliers to do what you ask, make clear the reason or positive impact it is making. Many tasks may seem mundane, such as analyzing data or keeping accurate attendance, but they are actually important to student achievement or a vital part of the business of school. For such tasks, make sure the importance is understood by all.

If a high flier perceives a task to be a waste of time, rethink it to see if he is right. Is the task necessary or do you need to explain it better? Involving your strongest teachers in the process of creating tasks or evaluating their effectiveness can also be helpful. If it is a district or state requirement that cannot be changed or tweaked, be clear about that. Sometimes it works to simply say something like, "We do this to stay out of trouble and off the radar."

How to Support High Fliers

High fliers need opportunities to develop their leadership and teaching skills. For them, professional development may need to take place outside of the building because in many areas they may be the top performer in the building and therefore have no one to learn from. If funds are available for travel to conferences, allocate these funds for the high fliers whenever possible. They can then come back and train others. Having high fliers become leaders in professional development training fosters their leadership abilities and can benefit their teaching.

While high fliers want to see that their abilities are appreciated, be careful not to overuse them. These teachers will often be courted by other schools and by the district to fill leadership and administrative positions. Help them feel valued (see Chapter 4) and make it clear to them what specifically about their performance is impressive to you. When you pick high-flying teachers to take on a leadership role, share with them why you did so. Be sure you are not going to them too often whenever you need extra help. While they would probably do any job you give them well, use them only for important jobs. If you need a family fun night planned and new curriculum created for new test standards, don't ask your high flier to do both. Get the high flier to develop the curriculum and another person to plan the event. This will help protect your high flier from burnout and will also help keep this valuable teacher with you longer.

Many of your high fliers will eventually leave for promotions or new leadership roles, and this is one of the accepted downsides to effectively helping develop leaders. But you want them to leave because it is a better opportunity for them to impact students, not because they feel unappreciated or overused.

Mid Fliers

The majority of teachers are mid fliers. This can be a more mixed group than high fliers and low fliers. It may include high fliers on their way down, mid fliers on their way up, low fliers who are responding well to support and improving their work, and those who always have been and always will be mid fliers. They can be responsive to criticism, and their level of contentment can range quite a bit from completely content with their current level to not content at all. These are generally the "go along to get along" type of people.

Mid fliers are also a valuable part of your staff. They can help foster student learning, but unlike the high fliers, they do need more support from administrators and instructional coaches in helping hone their craft. They tend to be steady in their classroom practice but less creative than high fliers. You know what you are going to find when you walk into their classrooms, and generally it will be good practice.

How to Communicate with Mid Fliers

Mid fliers tend not to need as much communication and explanation as high or low fliers. They tend to take in communication and move on without a lot of discussion. Because of this, it can sometimes be difficult to elicit the opinions of mid fliers, but since this is the majority of teachers, their opinion is of great importance. Giving them chances to share their ideas in small group settings or anonymously through surveys can help open up communication. Building relationships with them to let them know their opinion is valued can also help open them up to communication and participation in the shared leadership process. You can build these relationships by having conversations about classroom practices, ensuring the teachers have a place on the leadership team, and engaging with them during the social part of work, such as athletic events, luncheons, and afterschool activities.

How to Get Mid Fliers to Do What Is Needed

Mid fliers tend to do what needs to be done to keep things running because they want to see school culture improve and student achievement increase. It is best to make things clear, preferably in writing, and to offer a clear path for question asking. These teachers generally feel less comfortable asking questions than high or low fliers, so make it clear that asking questions is okay, and make it clear who they should ask. If getting clarification is not easy, mid fliers will often make mistakes without meaning to because they will just do the best they can with the information they have.

Teachers in this group tend to take criticism hard because they will attest that they are doing the best they can. When the best they can do is not good enough, they may resist trying to improve, citing that the expectations are unrealistic. If this happens, try to ascertain through conversations, meetings, or surveys what about the expectations feels unreachable to them or where they seem to struggle. Depending on what you learn, provide training, assign staff to work with teachers one-on-one or in small groups, give clearer directions, or modify the expectations.

How to Support Mid Fliers

Some teachers are at their peak when flying at the middle level, but others can improve with mentoring and targeted professional development. When you spot a mid flier with high-flier potential—perhaps because the teacher seems to be a self-starter, asks relevant questions about the school, or offers solutions to problems he sees—analyze the areas where the teacher needs improvement. Once you understand that, consider targeted mentoring with a teacher who is strong in the mid flier's areas of weakness or have the teacher go through specific professional development in those areas. Be upfront with teachers who have high-flier potential: let them know you think they have what it takes to really rise at your school with extra work. Having the encouragement and faith of the principal can mean a lot in these situations.

For the rest of the mid fliers, schoolwide professional development and chances to be involved in leadership in small ways are two ways to provide support. They do not typically need to be recognized as often as high fliers, but they still want to feel valued—though they tend to enjoy less-public ways of being involved or recognized. They are often willing to serve on committees and share their ideas, but rarely want to lead the committee or be the one to share the ideas of the committee with others.

Low Fliers

Low fliers will typically make up a small percentage of your teaching population, but in a school that has been under a weak administration for any extended period of time or is considered to be a difficult place to work, the percentage of these teachers could be higher. These teachers thrive where there is weak or limited supervision and will look for a principal who is uncomfortable with holding others accountable and who shies away from conflict.

These teachers are not necessarily difficult, argumentative, or troublesome. They simply want to do as little work as possible and not be bothered. They are often more concerned with earning a paycheck than teaching students. They tend to be defensive when given criticism, even if it is constructive, and tend to have reasons or excuses as to why their performance is poor to begin with. They will generally do what is asked, but they're likely to do the bare minimum, do it late, or do it incorrectly. They are generally content with their level and either they do not see that they are performing at that level or else they are not concerned about it.

Your focus in handling these chronically underperforming teachers is different from your focus with other teachers. Principals do not have the luxury of time, so you must accept that it is highly unlikely that these teachers will become high fliers, and while some will upgrade to mid fliers, this is less likely than mid fliers becoming high fliers. Low fliers aspire for mediocrity, and that is simply not good enough for your students. Once teachers establish themselves at this level, your best move is usually to document their status and counsel them into a different profession. The person might still be a low flier in the next position, whatever it might be, but a low-flying person in another job is likely less damaging for society than a low-flying teacher.

Of course you want to be careful not to be too quick to judge someone. Being a low flier, like being a mid or high flier, is not about performance on a particular task, but more about personality type and overall performance over an extended period of time. A high flier might struggle or make a mistake in a particular area, but would probably be deeply affected by this and work hard to never let it happen again. A low flier simply accepts the failure and either excuses it away or is not bothered by it. Look for "patterns of flight" before deciding the status of a particular teacher.

How to Communicate with Low Fliers

Communication with low fliers should be simple, direct, clear-cut, and in writing. These teachers are often looking for the easy way out, and "the directions weren't clear" is an easy way to excuse themselves out of poor performance. Some try to excuse their performance as misunderstandings and will devote their time to defending themselves and their performance instead of correcting the problem. Giving directions in writing, especially when you expect that there will be a performance issue, helps with documentation (see section entitled "LOW-PERFORMING EMPLOYEES").

If documenting poor performance, you may wish to limit who communicates with or gives directions to these teachers. This doesn't mean controlling at all times who talks with the underperforming teacher, but if the administrative team consists of multiple members, it may mean limiting who works directly with that person to avoid confusion. It is also important to have members of the administration talk frequently to one another, which helps prevent low performers from trying to play members of the team against one another. If you are working in a large school with many administrators, it is easy for some teachers to keep asking other administrators until they get the answer they want. Quality communication keeps such an unproductive environment from growing within the school.

How to Get Low Fliers to Do What Is Needed

Sometimes, no matter the support given, some teachers don't perform up to task. Give these employees opportunities to do what is needed and document when they do not. Make your directions very clear and put them in writing, then supervise closely to ensure that the work is done. These teachers need clear step-by-step directions and possibly someone to work with them depending on the importance of the task. If, after multiple opportunities—including one-on-one mentoring and all relevant training—a teacher continues to perform poorly in ways that can potentially damage the progress of your school, do not ask this teacher to get involved in important projects any more. Limit the work to the basic requirements of the job.

How to Support Low Fliers

A true low flier usually can't be changed, so it's best to document performance and eventually move the person out. The beginning of the documentation process should consist of you clearly telling the teacher what is wrong with the performance and giving clear direction about how to fix it. Not only is this the best way to give someone an opportunity to improve, but it makes expectations clear and deliberate.

Employees do not want to guess what the boss wants. Professional development targeted to the teacher's area of greatest weakness, on-going meetings with the principal or another member of the administrative team, or mentoring sessions with a teacher or teacher support staff are all ways to try to support the teacher early on. If the teacher does not respond, these attempts at support become part of your documentation of the weak performance.

Dealing with Difficult Staff

Difficult staff members are not necessarily difficult because of the quality of their teaching or their performance on job-related tasks. Difficult staff members are those who deliberately work against you to prevent your vision from being carried out. Most low-flying teachers are not troublesome or argumentative, and they generally stay out of the way. While they are not good for the education of students, they are, in fact, not difficult. Similarly, many talented high-flying teachers fail to submit lesson plans on time or march to the beat of their own drummer. These teachers may at times be challenging to supervise, but they are not difficult either.

Difficult staff may be difficult for any of a number of reasons. They may still feel loyalty to your predecessor, or they may be biased against your age, experience, race, or gender. They may simply believe they are right, and you are wrong. When you have difficult staff, don't take it personally. What's important is not your feelings or the teacher's, but what is best for students.

In a principal's first year (or years) at a school, it is very common to encounter some resistant staff members who seem determined to block any changes. These staff members can consume many hours of your time because they have the experience and knowledge to make things difficult for a new leader. They might do this by exploiting division among the staff that you didn't know existed or by purposely doing a task wrong. And it's possible that it may take weeks, months, and sometimes even years for you to discover who is sabotaging your initiatives.

The difficult staff members described in this chapter are not simply teachers who disagree on a particular issue, they are barriers to change and improvement. Many schools may have one, two, or maybe more difficult teachers who refuse to comply with district directives or schoolwide initiatives. They do not want to learn new ways to teach and are generally negative. Obviously, before labeling anyone as difficult, you will want to make many attempts to identify common ground, share philosophical beliefs, and debate pedagogy. It is part of your job to gather feedback and be persuasive about why a faculty member needs to adopt a particular practice.

Difficult staff members are often divided into two categories: those we know about and those we don't.

The Difficult Ones We Know About

Every school faculty seems to have a cantankerous employee or two. They may be unhappy outside of school or with their circumstances overall. Some do not even realize that their attitude has a negative impact on those around them, while others seem to pride themselves as being "courageous" enough to say what they claim "everyone else is afraid to say," even if the opinion is only their own.

> ### Stories from the Field
>
> **A brand new principal was appointed to a middle school after being moved up quickly, and she was noticeably younger than most of the teachers in the building. One teacher in particular was bothered by this and didn't think the principal had the ability to lead due to her age. In both large and small group settings, the teacher took every opportunity to question the decisions of the principal or make references to her age, even referring to her as a "young pup." The principal began to see that this was affecting others' views of her. The**

> principal called in the teacher along with another witness from the school's leadership team to discuss the teacher's inappropriate remarks and the effect those remarks were having on the school culture. The teacher was told that all remarks had to cease, any further remarks would be documented in her personnel file, and further action would be taken if necessary. While the teacher was never on board with the principal, she did stop making these remarks, and her negative effect on the school environment was mitigated.

Difficult teachers criticize publicly or purposely make mistakes that will get noticed. If you want different behavior from such a teacher, you must identify the root of the problem. Sometimes it is exactly what the teacher has been complaining about, but sometimes, as in the previous example, the teacher has an issue with you in general and will turn everything into a problem.

Honest, individual conversations are important when leading adults. This should stop some overt behavior for some staff members, but this can also increase the underground criticism, which isn't any better. Whether you directly engage these teachers will need to be decided on a case-by-case basis. Documenting your decisions and their effects is an important part of your growth as a principal. Addressing the behaviors directly can also provide the opportunity to invite the staff member to be part of the changes you are implementing.

When a gardener sets to work, he waters the flowers and not the rocks. Rocks simply get rolled out of the way before being completely removed from the garden. Teacher leaders who want to move forward in the school's direction are your flowers. Water them by sharing your attention and decision-making with those staff members. As for difficult staff members who are obstacles, the most immediate thing you can do is roll them out of the way. Remove them from leadership positions they have held; change their status quo by changing their roles, teaching assignments, or responsibilities; create new leadership teams that minimize or exclude those teachers. Limit their effectiveness by limiting both their influence and their access to knowledge.

However, some principals prefer to keep the difficult ones in leadership positions and try to cultivate relationships so they can closely observe them and more accurately document what the teachers are doing that is so difficult. This model can work, too. It depends on your style.

The Difficult Ones We Haven't Discovered Yet

Some difficult staff members are sly about being an obstacle to success. They will appear to be supportive in your presence but then destructive in your absence. These difficult teachers will eventually reveal themselves if you pay attention.

Principals, especially ones who are creating major change, must always be on the lookout for staff wanting to sabotage that change. Many teachers will show you who they are in overt ways, but others will be subtle. Once you start to notice that you may have difficult teachers, follow the steps for "The Difficult Ones We Know About." Otherwise, the in-house saboteurs will damage your efforts in ways that no outside person can.

Keep in mind that low fliers and saboteur groups represent a small minority of a teaching faculty. It would be a mistake to lead with paranoia, marginalizing the staff that you depend on to do the important work of educating children. Live by the old expression, "Be open-minded, but don't be so open-minded that your brain falls out." An effective principal must assess each staff member's strengths and weaknesses and expect that the great majority of a staff will work hard and with the best intentions.

***

Educators, by nature, are lifelong learners, and come to education from many paths. Some have had the calling to be teachers from a young age; others come to education later in life, perhaps because they want to give something back. Regardless of whether a teacher is new or a veteran with decades in the classroom, helping them hone and master their craft is a top priority for you. Your support of teachers will impact student achievement and growth.

Being the principal means making tough, difficult calls regarding personnel. At times, this means helping teachers realize that this career might not be what they are best suited for. One of your highest priorities, if not your very highest, is making sure that competent teachers are in the classroom to help children grow intellectually, socially, and emotionally. You will achieve this goal by providing professional development, placing teachers in the position to be successful, and helping shepherd teachers through the changes the school will undergo as you work to make improvements.

CHAPTER SEVEN

Leading Change

New principals will inevitably make changes when they start at a new school, and even veteran principals will often make tweaks to continually improve their school. While some changes are insignificant, like when faculty meetings are scheduled, others are more drastic, such as changing a teacher evaluation process to include standardized test results. Bigger changes can be difficult for those impacted, and resistance to change is a common defense mechanism as people try to protect what they know rather than gamble on the unknown.

> ## Stories from the Field
>
> **A principal was appointed to a "failing" high school that needed significant changes. Historically, the master schedule was created by the department heads selecting who would teach each class in their department. This system was seniority-based, and as a result, teachers with longevity were assigned to the honors classes—the classes without a high-stakes test and with students who were deemed easier**

> to teach. Teachers new to the school were assigned the freshmen classes, the difficult high-stakes classes, and whatever classes were left over.
>
> The new principal explained that it was her job to match talent with need, and teachers could share input about their preferences; however, she would be making the final decisions. Several senior teachers resisted this change because they considered the master schedule their right and responsibility. This was a big change, the principal explained, but a necessary one, especially in light of the "failing" designation according to state standards. Despite resistance, the principal stood her ground.

In this example, as is often the case in the change process, the key to helping the teachers through this paradigm shift was consistency. Had the principal allowed some teachers or departments to choose their schedules, it would have seemed like disparate treatment, and that would have resulted in others not taking the new principal at her word.

A Leader's Character

Some changes are philosophical while others are procedural. In either case, the leader needs to adhere to three critical principles: transparency, accepting responsibility, and sharing leadership. These principles form the backbone of strong character.

Transparency

Transparency means explaining the rationale for your decisions and explicitly communicating that rationale so there's little room for misunderstanding. Essentially, principals need to make public their thought process about why something is or isn't being done. This doesn't mean you have to explain every decision in detail, but as a general rule, if stakeholders know that it is acceptable to ask why, the intimidation level of the principalship decreases, and stakeholders are more likely to ask questions rather than harbor suspicions.

When you lead with transparency, it helps ease the worries of those who lack power to guide decisions. Keep in mind that it is not enough for you to think you are being transparent; the employees, students, and parents must also think so. Just as you are not communicating if the person you are talking to does not understand you, you are not being transparent if those around you do not see you that way.

Part of what helps build transparency is consistency. Employees would prefer to deal with a boss who is always cranky instead of one who is sometimes cranky. That lack of predictability means that if an employee waits for the "right" time to make a request, an answer that might be a no could sometimes be a yes. This is not effective leadership.

To be consistent, you must have policies, best practices, and guiding principles that are not impacted by your personal situation or mood.

> ### Stories from the Field
>
> A principal with a history of being a transparent leader received a report of a gun in the school being held in a purple backpack. He conducted a lockdown and went room to room in search of the purple backpack. Teachers knew it was not a drill once it lasted longer than five minutes, so the principal needed to provide some information. However, rather than be completely transparent and explain what he was looking for and why, the principal emailed that the lockdown would continue until the investigation was completed.
>
> The principal conducted the search, and when it was over, in a faculty meeting—not via email—he explained what actually happened. He explained that he couldn't risk sharing the concern about the purple backpack in an email that could have inadvertently been

> projected for all students to see in a classroom. The owner of the backpack could have panicked and tried to conceal the weapon. This could have turned a gun in a backpack into a gun being handled, which is far more dangerous. Teachers understood the logic, and in future situations were more willing to trust the principal's judgment.

This principal was not 100 percent transparent at first. However, he had a history of transparency, and because he explained to the staff his rationale in this particular situation, his staff were willing to trust his judgment. If you establish yourself as transparent and honest, your staff will do the same. Share your reasoning for decisions you make whenever possible. Of course some staff members will doubt you even when you're being honest, but you'll have even more doubters when you are vague.

Being transparent does not mean sharing all information at all times. In some situations you cannot be transparent, as is the case with human resources issues. However, trust is built when you consistently share the information you can.

Here are some guidelines for establishing yourself as transparent and trustworthy:
- **Tell the truth.** You may not always be able to tell everything, but you never need to lie.

If you can't reveal something, don't say anything.
- **Explain the rationale for your decisions.** This is important, because explaining the decision-making process reveals various considerations you had to weigh that others may not have been aware of.
- **Share information with everyone in a stakeholder group.** If you need to explain a change to teachers, explain it to all teachers. Don't send an email or a memorandum to a select few. When everyone receives information at the same time, that shows equity—and that breeds trust.

Responsibility

The principal gets to make mistakes in front of audience. Just like slipping on ketchup at the mall food court, mistakes can be embarrassing. However, effective leaders handle mistakes the way they handle everything else: head on and with transparency. Part of a principal's guiding principles—which should be communicated to all who will listen—is "At our school, we won't always do the right things, but we will do things for the right reasons." Covering up or minimizing puts the principal's character in question and leads to distrust.

Stories from the Field

A student with special needs who was supposed to be supervised at all times got hurt because the person supervising him became distracted helping another student. While the mistake was not the principal's, principals are the face of the school and thus are often in the position to accept blame or credit. When the local news interviewed the principal, she discussed the situation from a point of sorrow that the child was hurt. She didn't blame the child or employee or act as if it was an unavoidable circumstance. The principal said, "We are so sorry that Malik was hurt, and we are investigating how this occurred so we can put measures in place to ensure this doesn't happen again. We have discussed the situation with Malik's family and are hopeful for a quick recovery."

Accepting responsibility is an essential part of leadership, and employees appreciate when you are not quick to pass the blame, even when it might be deserved. Some leaders are quick to fold under this type of intense pressure, but effective leaders stick to the truth and learn from every mistake so they do not repeat them.

Shared Leadership

Shared leadership, which is discussed in detail in Chapter 4, does not mean a school must be run like a democracy. Some decisions need to be made by the principal. However, many decisions can be made with input from the people affected, and it is those decisions that need to be shared. For instance, budgeting should be understood by all rather than created in secret by the principal. This does not mean you are not involved in decisions or that you just wait until the end to approve or not approve them; rather, you're a member of a representative team. Ultimately, you have the final say, but an effective leader recognizes when others have a better idea or solution. Sharing power does not mean conceding authority to others, but through the process of bringing others into the conversation, a leader helps foster buy-in while exponentially increasing creativity in making decisions that improve schools.

Occasionally, principals involve others in decisions for which they already have an outcome planned. Others see through this, and it is poor practice. First, teachers value their time as one of their most important resources, and they do not appreciate having it wasted. Second, having people contribute ideas when they are not really needed or agree with you regardless of their own opinions is not shared leadership.

Historically speaking, schools had a hierarchal and bureaucratic way of operating using a top-down approach. Today, many schools have modernized like businesses in creating teams to effectively deal with issues that arise. This is not to say that you cannot set guidelines or highlight areas of emphasis, but it does mean that people who are part of the team are equal members. Make sure that leadership team members understand that discourse is healthy and that no member's opinion is more important than anyone else's. It is critical that you emphasize that the point of meeting isn't just so people agree with you. The purpose of shared leadership is to develop synergy and make the best decisions possible for the school community.

A Leader's Style

As a new leader, it's important to know your leadership style and strengths to best lead your school. By understanding your strengths and weaknesses, you can hone and develop your leadership skills. No one style fits every leadership position—and no leader should rely on just one style—but knowing where your strengths lie will help you lead effectively. And sharing this information will help your followers[2]

---

[2] Followers are members of the school and community who believe in what you're doing and actively support

know best how to approach and communicate with you. Honest discussions about leadership styles and learning the strengths and weaknesses of followers will help you build a leadership team that complements your leadership style.

> ### Stories from the Field
>
> A new principal met with his staff for the first time. Having been an assistant principal prior to this appointment, he was armed with analysis of his personality traits and a list of his strengths and weaknesses as a leader based on inventory tests. He talked candidly with the staff about his leadership traits. Having learned about his predecessor from the central office and in talks with him, the new principal highlighted differences in order to make sure the teachers knew what to expect compared to the predecessor. The new principal had also sent surveys to the staff with specific questions about what they look for in a leader. He used this information to highlight the differences between the two principals so the staff would see them as two different people.

you. Cultivating followers is an important part of your change process.

These conversations and fact-finding measures take time but are vital in building an effective leadership team and rapport with staff. Understanding what style teachers are used to coupled with understanding your own strengths and weaknesses as a leader will help you know what leadership style to use and what areas to develop.

If you need help understanding your leadership style, strengths, and weaknesses, talk with someone you trust to give you honest feedback. Someone who has mentored you is a good choice. You can also take a leadership inventory; search online for one that you like, or ask a librarian to help you choose a book.

In addition to your own leadership style, it is important to find out the leadership style of your superior in order to know how to work with her. Of course you should stay true to yourself, but be adaptable in working with supervisors who might have a different style from yours. For example, you can be very direct and open with your staff, and for the most part they will learn to adapt to that. However, if your supervisor does not respond well to directness, it will be very difficult to communicate that way with her. As the subordinate, you have to learn to work with your supervisor's style.

Stories from the Field

> A middle school principal was assigned a new supervisor. Almost immediately, the principal felt communication was strained because she recognized that the supervisor was not comfortable communicating via email. The principal would email documents and questions, and the supervisor would call her in response to the email. Finally, the duo discussed the situation. The supervisor explained that he had a no-email policy; he believed emailing put him in a position of increased scrutiny and so he simply did not compose emails. As quirky as it seemed, the principal had to learn to adapt to this. Over time, the supervisor and the principal developed a mutually respectful relationship where they were able to communicate effectively.

This scenario highlights another adage for the principal: You must learn which battles to fight and where to draw the proverbial line in the sand. This goes back to your guiding principle: Is the issue harmful to children? Does it interfere with the vision of the school? For example, maybe you have a preference for a copy machine company based on years of good service, but the district has decided to switch all schools to a different copier company. This change may not be what you want, but it does not hurt students. If it does not interfere with teaching and learning, it is unlikely to be a battle worthy of your time.

Delegating

Sometimes, especially when implementing change, you will feel compelled to micromanage everything you are responsible for as the leader of the school. This is not practical, though, given the volume of responsibility you are faced with. Instead, develop a system for delegating so you can effectively handle the really important tasks and avoid being waylaid by time-consuming tasks that do not carry the same weight. To fairly and equally divvy up delegated tasks, you'll need to learn the job responsibilities of your followers and staff.

Delegation is also paramount in developing effective leadership abilities in teachers and assistant principals who aspire to leadership roles. You were groomed somewhere along the way or you would not be in this position today. When deciding what and how to delegate to your own followers, reflect back on how others helped and delegated to you. Be sure not to overload any eager, aspiring leaders with too much responsibility before they are ready.

Once you have established your system of delegation, you will have achieved two important feats: the ability to handle your workload and the development of leaders within your own followers.

How do you know what to delegate and what to hold onto? Consider these guiding principles.

Have You Done This Before?

The first time a task must be done it is usually best for you to do it yourself so you have the experience of doing it. Once you've completed something from start to finish, you are better prepared to delegate it to someone else because you understand the time, effort, and skills it takes. On the other hand, if you delegate a task without ever having completed it, you will not understand the demands the task requires. You cannot check progress because you will not know what to check for.

For example, if you leave oversight of the computer system for running report cards to someone else without understanding how to run it, you will never understand this important task and will not know if the report cards have been run properly.

In addition, when you delegate a task without understanding it, you are dependent on others to get that task done. Assistant principals, secretaries, and teachers come and go, and if you must rely on someone else to get information or do something for you, you are setting yourself up to be taken advantage of—or to be stuck when the person you depend on is not there. You need to be able to depend on your own knowledge and experience. If you cannot or do not think you can handle the computer system, for instance, others will doubt your competency with this and other topics. Find a trusted, competent person to show you how it works.

This means that first-year principals have many duties to do, making your first year very tiring. The good news is that this makes the rest of your career much easier because you'll understand the processes you assign to others.

Does This Have to Be Handled by the Principal?

Schools have many teachers and sometimes more than one assistant principal but only one principal. The principal should do the jobs no one else can do. Evaluating assistant principals or instructional coaches is a principal job. Having them evaluated by outside people reduces your influence over the behavior you wish to see, and allowing one assistant principal to evaluate the others (or assistant principals to evaluate coaches) can sometimes lead to unnecessary strife between the different parties.

There is a reason the principal works more days, more hours and gets paid more money. You're responsible for tasks that cannot be done by any other staff member. For example, you have to be the final stop in the purchasing cycle—not the *only* stop, just the final stop. Teams can meet and make requests, budgets can be developed, and leadership can be shared, but before funds are expended, someone has to make sure there is money in the account to cover that expenditure. That someone is you. No one will excuse you for someone else's bookkeeping error—not the central office, not the auditors. Bill paying is not something to delegate.

So, what is? If you have done a task and understand it and a mistake in that task will not result in a catastrophe, then consider delegating it. Good items to delegate include running grade-level meetings, leading groups of teachers by grade level or department, athletics, curriculum, textbook distribution, and discipline. When you delegate, it does not mean that you totally hand off something. You must still supervise the process. However, each school only has one principal and the more you can spend your time doing the jobs only you can do, the more efficient you can be.

Getting Through the Implementation Dip

Change within an organization can be difficult for those who work there. Some people will be confused by it, some will be resistant, and it is not uncommon for leaders to feel like they're taking two steps backward for every step forward.

When change is introduced, it is inevitably followed by a drop in performance as employees go through a learning curve or the initial resistance to the change. We call this the **implementation dip.** If you're not prepared for it, the implementation dip can cause you to falter or give up on a change completely. Therefore you'll want to explain the implementation dip to your stakeholders. Be realistic about what you expect to see and how long you are going to stay the course before evaluating if the change needs to be modified or dropped completely. Being realistic and communicating clearly are two ways to steer through the implementation dip to the improvement that waits on the other side.

When in the implementation dip, leaders sometimes become frightened by it and abandon the change in favor of something that feels better or more comfortable. This is a mistake for two reasons. First, schools are made up of real people, and real people who are being stretched to improve will feel growing pains. It is natural, and you should not mistake growing pains for a sign that your plan is wrong. Second, when you abandon a change initiative, you send a message that you fear the change process and are ill-equipped to lead others through it.

This is one of the more challenging things for a school leader to learn: when to stay the course and when to make a mid-course correction. Sometimes you do need to abandon a change. However, only do so when it has been determined that one of the following is true. The change is:
- causing more harm than the status quo
- overwhelmingly not supported by those who are impacted by it
- opposed by those who rarely complain

The latter reason is particularly compelling. We know that some people will always be more vocal in general—they tend to complain openly, loudly, and often. However, many people don't want to rock the boat. These people are generally willing to accept changes due to their flexibility and ability to tolerate ambiguity. When these people come to you with a concern, you are wise to listen. They may even represent the silent majority. These same people are great candidates to help you adapt or modify your plan so it can be successful.

Stories from the Field

An overcrowded high school had a problem with hallway congestion. The principal decided to divert foot traffic that came through the cafeteria in another direction. In explaining the

change to the students, he said that a certain doorway was now "an invisible wall" during a certain time period in the day. He laid out options other than walking through that doorway to avoid the foot traffic jam.

Even though a teacher was posted on either side of the invisible wall, students tried to walk through it and questioned why they could not, because there was clearly an open doorway. After a week of conflict about the invisible wall, during which students increasingly challenged the invisible wall and complained to parents, the principal developed a different plan to ease traffic concerns and announced that the doorway was no longer an invisible wall.

The principal in this scenario was wise to discontinue the invisible wall because, although it may have been a good concept, it was not worth the high cost to implement—particularly in negative interactions between students and staff. The principal was not experiencing an implementation dip so much as the failure of a policy. When you have widespread resistance to a change, make the needed fix and move on rather than digging in your heels and making the situation worse.

What to Change First

In a perfect world, you would get a semester or year to observe and reflect before being called on to make changes. This would allow for adequate time to research the history behind the status quo, examine best practice, and identify how strong the support is for an alternative. However, principals are not given that luxury. Many things require swift changing because they are wrong or inconsistent with best practice. They may even be the reason the previous principal was removed. But you cannot show up on the first day and change everything, so how do you know what to change first?

Start with your guiding principle: If students are suffering, the practice cannot continue. Next, consider whether the status quo is legal, moral, ethical, and consistent with policy. And, finally, consider how student learning is being impacted. Your first changes should be to fix any issues that most strongly violate your guiding principle and essential standards.

> ### Stories from the Field
>
> **An assistant principal was promoted to principal in the same middle school, so she knew that students being tardy was a big problem. To combat the tardiness issue, she decided in her first week to eliminate the "warning bell,"**

which rang a minute before the tardy bell. She believed, and assumed that others agreed, that the warning bell did little more than give students license to stand in the hallway and chat until they heard it. The principal didn't think this change would be controversial, and she made the change without any discussion. She thought she was helping teachers and students by encouraging students to monitor their own time, just like in the real world, because "there are no warning bells in life."

This became a big battle for the principal. Without warning bells, students continued to be tardy, but now they blamed the lack of a warning bell. Teachers were confused about which bell was the final bell, and teachers and students began to lose even more instructional time arguing about tardiness and trying to track the time spent in the hallways. This caused teachers to complain privately and openly, which got back to parents, who joined the teachers in wanting the bells back.

This change was made at the wrong time. Tardiness did not hurt children and was not a violation of legal, moral, or ethical standards. The issue did need to be addressed, but the principal would likely have had better success if she'd done it at a later time and explained it ahead of time. As a new principal, she created unnecessary strife and unified the students, teachers, and parents against her. Making this change in the first week, with no warning and little dialogue, immediately made people fear that this would be symbolic of other changes to come.

***

It is important to recognize that the change process can create a wide range of emotions for all involved. Change, by its nature, is welcomed by some and resisted by others. If you have clear and specific reasons for your changes, and you communicate those reasons effectively, you'll have more who welcome than resist the changes. Don't stop that communication at the initial implementation, but continue throughout the process so everyone is aware of the progress being made. That can alleviate some of the anxiety surrounding change and keep all employees focused on making it work. Stay true to yourself and let your actions be guided by what is in the best interest of your students.

CHAPTER EIGHT

Documenting

The job of the principalship is so demanding and requires such multitasking that it is easy to feel like you're doing everything and accomplishing nothing. When you have time to reflect about the conversations you've had, promises you've made, warnings or commendations you've given, observations you've performed, and meetings you've attended, it's easy for all these situations to run together in your mind. And when you see a parent in the hallway on Thursday who greets you with, "I am Johnny's mom, and I thought about what you said yesterday..." you may feel panicked, thinking "Who's Johnny? What did we talk about?"

It does not inspire confidence in parents if you require them to remind you who their children are and what it was you said yesterday. Similarly, teachers and students will be reluctant to trust you or follow you if you are unable to recall what you've talked about with them, forget to fulfill promises you've made, or appear uninformed about issues that are important to them. You're the principal. You have to keep track of everything you do and say in a way that makes conversations and details easy to recall.

Because you supervise a staff, a building, and a student body, you also have to keep track of your leadership decisions, disciplinary decisions, and policy decisions—including why you made them. And sometimes you will need to quickly recover documents, emails, or phone call details if you are subpoenaed over legal matters regarding students or staff. Being able to produce, efficiently and specifically, the details of a conversation or steps that were taken regarding an employee or student—in some cases years in the past—will not only save you time but will often protect you when complaints are filed against you or the school.

In order to stay on top of everything, as well as to keep proof of discussions, events, and processes for later use, you need an easy-to-use and reliable system for documentation. This chapter shows you how and what to document.

How to Document

Documentation can be done in many ways. You may want to use a physical system, like a notebook and file folders, an electronic system, or—more likely—a combination of both. Here are some suggestions.

Composition Book

With this old-fashioned and reliable system, you can simply journal your activities on a day-by-day basis. Use a composition book, a series of legal pads, or just notebook paper in a binder. Any of the options is perfect for documenting details. You can carry the composition book with you and document throughout the day, which is beneficial because, especially in your first year, waiting too long between when something happens and when you document it can lead to forgetting important details. If you don't want to carry the notebook around with you, keep it on your desk where you can add to it throughout the day, and make it a part of your end-of-day routine to review what you have written and add in any details.

Another part of your end-of-the-day routine can be planning what needs to be done for tomorrow. In this way, the notebook can double as your daily to-do list.

Be sure to date every entry in these books or pads and store them in chronological order so they're easy to go back to. You may also want to have different notepads for different areas to help you keep track. For instance, one notepad for day-to-day items and general notes, one for teacher observations, one for notes from weekly meetings with teachers, and one for notes from interviews. This can make it easier when going back to look up information.

Weekly Date Book

Another option is using a weekly date book. You can find these in any office supply store. The dates come preprinted, and as you have meetings, teacher observations, parent phone calls, etc., you can write the name, subject, and a few key details on the designated date. Bonus tip: By highlighting people's names, you can more easily find them as you thumb through to recall previous contacts with a person. When highlighting, consider a color-coded system. For example, yellow for parent/student interactions, orange for teacher interactions, and green for community interactions. For contacts that are more "fragile" than others—for example, the superintendent, a board member, or your supervisor—place a colored sticky note over the date.

Stories from the Field

A principal's supervisor called to discuss a few things. During the call, the principal explained that an effective teacher had recently had a baby and needed to arrive at work 10 minutes later each day due to when the baby's childcare center opened. The supervisor and principal agreed that allowing the teacher to have first period as her planning period would solve this problem.

> The conversation ended, and the principal documented the conversation.
>
> Six months later, when visiting the school, the principal's supervisor noticed the teacher entering the school later than required and asked the principal about it. The principal reminded the supervisor about their discussion, but the supervisor didn't remember it. They walked back to the principal's office, where he retrieved the documentation and reviewed not only that decision, but the other important points they discussed that day. This jogged the supervisor's memory, and she apologized for doubting the principal in the first place.

Some employees may be uncomfortable knowing that you keep detailed notes about interactions. Don't let that dissuade you from doing what you need to do. Those who express discomfort may be communicating that they benefit from vague leadership and ambiguity. But such vagueness is not effective supervision of employees. Operate under the assumption that professionals want to do the right thing, and detailed documentation helps keep you organized and keeps everyone a little more honest.

Electronic Journals

You can use a journal or note-taking application (such as Day One, Capture 365 Journal, or Evernote) similar to the way you would use a composition notebook or datebook. You can choose from many options for Mac and PC, and most are inexpensive or free and easy to use. Many offer password protection, which you'll need if others have access to your computer, and most sync with a cloud and automatically back up. If you prefer something simpler, use a word processing application with a detailed filing system for documents.

Email Yourself

For lengthier details, some principals like to send an email to themselves, which you can do from anywhere if you have a smartphone. This method provides a date and time stamp, which can be very useful if later you have to prove something happened and when. Some principals like to use this strategy when documenting performance issues of staff members. For example: "While at morning bus duty, I noticed Ms. Fishburn pull into the parking lot 15 minutes late." This may be a one-time event and never become a significant issue, but, if it occurs on a regular basis, the documentation has already begun. You need only print the email and place it in the employee's personnel folder so that it is easily found later. Emails to yourself can easily be pasted into an electronic journal, too, if you want to keep everything in one place.

Email Systems and Other Electronic Efficiency

Good leaders respond to all emails they receive, but that can be a challenge when faced with the volume you receive as a principal. You'll need to establish a system that works for you. Some principals try to answer all emails as soon as they read them throughout the day, while others read them and wait until they have some sustained time in front of the computer to respond. We recommend a combination of the two. Read all emails as you get them (or as soon as possible) and respond to those that you can do quickly. Mark all other emails as unread, and respond to those when you have time to sit and collect your thoughts.

Return all emails (and phone calls) within a 24-hour period. Even if you are not able to fully respond to an email, at least let the person know you have received it and that you are working on the situation. Give an estimate of when the person can expect a more detailed response. For instance, suppose a parent asks you if his child, who has been given an opportunity to be an exchange student, can complete coursework online with your school district at the same time.

You may need to contact someone at the district level to find out the answer, so email the parent to let him know that and give a date when you will contact him again.

Keeping track of these emails and responses is a vital requirement of the principal's job since so much of today's communication occurs electronically. Model this responsiveness to your faculty and staff and expect the same from them.

It's also critical to keep those voluminous emails organized. Most email programs allow for the creation of folders to file received and sent emails. You may want to establish separate folders for teachers, other staff, discipline issues, family communications, communications with superiors, and media communications. You can break down each of these folders into more precise subfolders for individuals in each category. Your system can be as intricate as you prefer.

Remember that the purpose is to be able to find the emails in a timely manner if asked for information. You may want to have few folders so that you don't spend time trying to decide if an email sent to your boss and a parent belongs in family communications or communication with superiors. Or you may prefer the higher detail that dozens of folders provide. Most email systems also have a search feature so you can look for emails from certain people or about a particular topic. If yours does, use it, and consider organizing your emails in a way that works well with the search options. For instance, if you can search the subject lines of emails, but not the text within the body of the email, make sure you put keywords in all email subject lines. If you use a cloud system, you can access all these folders from anywhere.

> **IMPORTANT**
>
> When emailing yourself about someone else, a common mistake is to put the person you're emailing about in the "To" field of the email. Making this error is not only embarrassing but also puts you in an awkward—and potentially very difficult—position with the recipient of the email. This is why it is so important not only to pay attention when corresponding, but also to make sure all your communication is professional. In the example in section entitled "Electronic Journals – Email Systems and Other Electronic Efficiency" about Ms. Fishburn being late, it would be unwise to include speculation about why Ms. Fishburn is late: "While at morning bus duty, I noticed Ms. Fishburn pull into the parking lot 15 minutes late. She was probably out late at the bar she loves so much watching the game." This is not professional and is not based in fact. In addition, if you accidentally send the email to Ms. Fishburn, she likely would be dismayed by the commentary. State only facts and logical conclusions drawn from those facts. For example, "Ms. Fishburn was 15 minutes,

> so her students were likely not being supervised at the time" is an example of a logical conclusion.

Besides email, every school administrator should have access to a scanner to transfer and save paper documents as electronic files in order to save space. For example, after open house sign-in sheets are complete, scan them and save the electronic document for school improvement team meetings, Title I purposes, and so on.

Organizing electronic folders is important and can be simple for principals. Create a separate folder for each school year with subfolders inside for typical categories such as school opening, school closing, data, testing, recommendations, reprimands, and weekly newsletters. This way it's easy to refer back to something so you don't have to reinvent the wheel. For example, you can refer back to your "Event Scheduling" folder to see how you've handled breakfast on the half day before the winter holidays so you can handle it the most efficient way this year. These folders can also be very useful if you move to a new school. You'll find that although the names have changed, the essential organizational items are the same.

With regard to electronic files, it goes without saying that you need to back everything up. An external hard drive is a reliable way to do this, but a hard drive can be lost or stolen or damaged just like a computer can. More and more, a good cloud service such as iCloud or Dropbox is the way to go. In addition to storing your files safely off site, it also makes these files available from other devices at any time. The best recommendation is to back up your files on a regular basis (monthly or every 6 weeks at a minimum) and back them up in multiple ways if possible. (Your district may recommend services or procedures for doing this.)

What to Document

It's important to keep documentation in four main areas: interactions, best practices, elements of shared leadership, and employee performance.

Document Your Interactions

Most principals have at least a couple dozen staff members and some principals have hundreds. These employees will come to you for advice or a decision on a regular basis (and often, it will seem, at the same time). Consider the following typical interactions:
- A teacher asks about the best date to schedule school pictures.
- Someone else inquires about the plan for recess considering the rainy forecast.

- The cafeteria manager wants to know if it is okay to schedule the meal for Grandparents' Day on Monday rather than Tuesday.
- Another teacher wonders if it would be okay to take her son to the orthodontist instead of attending the faculty meeting today.
- A new teacher needs clarity about district assessment practices.
- The librarian asks to schedule the book fair.
- The football coach warns you about an angry parent who will be calling.
- The bookkeeper needs a written response about an audit finding.
- The custodians express concern that kids with their wheelie sneakers are scratching the wax on the floors.
- The school resource officer wants to conduct a lockdown drill for safety.
- The district maintenance worker needs a key to a location only you have access to.
- A teacher calls to tell you that the Internet just went down, which means he cannot take attendance electronically.

It's not unrealistic to imagine encountering all these interactions—or similar ones—within the first hour or two of coming to school.

With all this going on every day, you absolutely must document the things you have said to others. Knowing what you decided or didn't decide, or what you promised or was promised to you—these are key pieces of information you need to be able to recall easily. Amnesia can be an inevitable unintended consequence of doing too much too often, but if you are often responding to stakeholders by saying "I do not recall," they will deduce that they cannot trust you, and even your best intentions will be misunderstood.

This kind of documentation is incredibly important in dealing with voice mails and phone calls. Most people who call a principal want an immediate response. Parents in particular have good reason to expect a short response time. You are responsible for the most important people to them: their children. Worried parents are not going to be satisfied to wait longer just because you are busy, and one of the most common complaints parents have is that their messages are not returned.

To stay on top of phone communication, document every phone call and voice mail that comes in by recording it in your composition book, electronic diary, or whatever method you're using. Note the events as soon as you can after they conclude. These notes can be brief and simple, for example, "Approved Ms. Brown to go on field trip with English teachers for extra supervision" or "Mr. Chu indicated he would be out for knee surgery in March" or "Reminded Ms. Gonzalez to be on hall duty until 8:23 daily." For phone calls, it can be as simple as, "I called

Mr. Thompson at 555-1212 at 12:40p.m. on Wednesday and left a voicemail message. Was that the correct number?"

Using shorthand, such as left message (LM), no answer (NA), or returned call (RC) along with the date and time can protect you from accusations that you are not returning calls. The point of this documentation is not to create more work; it is simply to cite what work you're doing and remind yourself what you have agreed to.

Document Best Practices

The school world is a cyclical place. Graduation and field day come annually, as does spring testing. You'll save yourself a lot of time and extra work by documenting how you organized these events and noting what worked well and what did not. Otherwise, every year is like doing that task for the first time. For example, a high school principal might have a physical or an electronic folder marked "Homecoming" that cites dates and times and any pitfalls from the year before. The "Testing" folder may have reminders like, "the math test always takes longer than any other test because staff need to distribute and collect calculators."

Documenting these reminders ensures that you don't repeat your own mistakes or get surprised by things again and again. It also allows you to repeat things that worked especially well so that prep time decreases year to year—or at least does not increase.

Document Shared Leadership

In the shared leadership process, you are regularly asking for feedback from teachers. In order for all teachers to truly feel heard, document how their input helped you arrive at your decisions and share that documentation with them. This can be done in emails, in faculty meetings, or in small group meetings. If feedback is gathered in a meeting rather than in writing, have someone take minutes and share those with the faculty.

YOUR COMMITMENT TO SHARED LEADERSHIP

In schools, it is not uncommon for stakeholders—students, parents, or staff—to approach the principal claiming to be speaking on behalf of themselves and others. Generally, however, these people are speaking only for themselves, because other individuals will make their voices known when an issue is important to them. Again, documentation will be important. Use a survey or solicit input in other ways to find out what the majority actually thinks, and then share that information with the staff, parents, or students along with your reactions. This not only documents their input, but it also documents that you asked for and heard their opinions—very important when creating buy-in.

> ### Stories from the Field
>
> A school began a new professional development initiative that required 10 hours per month of teacher time beyond the school day. The principal participated in the activities, and they seemed meaningful and helpful to teachers; however, a teacher who rarely complained mentioned that everyone on staff resented the additional time commitment.
>
> The principal sent a short anonymous survey to the staff to gauge perceptions. After gathering responses, the principal shared the results with the staff: 60 percent agreed the training was beneficial and worth the time, 20 percent thought it was not, and 20 percent marked "unsure." While 60 percent did not represent unanimity, it did indicate that the majority felt positively about the training, and "everyone" did not resent the extra time.

Taking the time to gather feedback and sharing the summary data with respondents demonstrates a documented commitment to shared leadership. It says, "I want to know what you think about this issue," which matters to teachers. Documentation and sharing are equally important in such cases to show you are listening and that you are being responsive.

STAKEHOLDER INPUT

Documenting what stakeholders think is very important when considering a policy change that will impact parents and students. For example, in some communities, the student dress code is a lightning rod issue on which principals feel like they are wrong regardless of what they decide. Sometimes, parents will agree to support a dress code that, when implemented, their children resist. When the dress code begins to cause discord at home, parents may withdraw their support and complain. As principals, we cannot change policy based on parental whims. This is when the documentation of shared leadership can be so important. Show parents the documented support they originally expressed for the policy and ask them to be patient as you all wait to see if the benefits you envisioned materialize.

IMPORTANT

Do not ask for feedback about something that you cannot or will not change. Nothing annoys people more than giving feedback and seeing nothing done with it or thinking that the responses will fall on deaf ears.

> Additionally, don't ask for feedback if you do not want it.

In the midst of controversy, distributing the feedback gained by shared leadership documentation will not always calm the detractors, but it generally will remind the logical, rational majority about why the change was implemented. If you can get the backing of that group, you can stay the course and work out specific problems rather than drop the initiative altogether.

Documenting shared leadership is also very helpful when defending current practice to your supervisors, who are charged with following up on complaints. Those who launch complaints to the district supervisors may portray a more serious problem than really exists in order to garner the support of your supervisor. The person complaining could be a poorly performing teacher or a parent who is upset with a particular teacher or policy. It is common for those who are complaining over your head to want to cast the situation in the most negative light possible with the hope of getting the policy, decision, or practice reversed. Documentation can inoculate you from such overblown claims. For example, when a teacher makes a complaint and asserts that "all of the teachers" feel the same way, you can show evidence of what teachers really think based on objective feedback.

THE HAWD? (HOW ARE WE DOING?) PROCESS

While documenting feedback on specific topics is necessary in shared leadership, you need a way to get feedback on a regular basis and keep your finger on the pulse of the school. Once again, it is not enough to just document that you have asked for feedback—you must also document what you are doing with the feedback and why you made the decisions you did.

For example, we use what we call our HAWD? (How Are We Doing?) process four times a year to make sure we have identified and solved any problems. In the third week of school, staff members are invited to meet with the executive principal during their planning periods. HAWD? is optional, so not all teachers choose to participate. During the meetings, staff members discuss what is going well and what needs to be improved. If the same issue is mentioned two or more times, it is included on a summary sheet that is published for all employees along with an "action taken" plan for solving the identified problem.

The HAWD? process has proven valuable time and again when problems are identified that most staff assumed the principal was already aware of. For example, teachers commented that the copy machine in the library was regularly out of order. In reality, it went out of order once but was never fixed—everyone assumed someone else reported the issue. The HAWD? process enables a school staff to work together to solve problems without the mystery of a suggestion box or fears of retaliation. Employee morale increases when everyone has a stake in making our school a better place to work.

The HAWD? process in the second quarter of school is organized into individual and group meetings (as determined by the participants themselves), and we share the results in the same way. In the third quarter, we solicit feedback through an anonymous survey, again sharing the results with all staff, and at the end of the year HAWD? is used for planning for the upcoming year.

Having a voice and seeing action in response to one's suggestions is a powerful morale builder for teachers, but if you do not document and show others that you are making specific changes based on their suggestions, the power of what you are doing can be lost. One of the most important messages the HAWD? process sends is that we can solve our own problems without layers of bureaucracy and fears of retaliation for those who communicate concerns. The process is similar to one that might be used in a family or a marriage (although far more formalized) in which family members say, "When _____ happens, I feel_____, and it is preventing me from doing my work because of_____."

Document Employee Performance

Documentation of employee performance falls into two main areas: a standard employee evaluation and a low-performing employee evaluation.

EMPLOYEE EVALUATION

In our current education climate, teacher evaluation is becoming increasingly important. Not long ago, teacher evaluation was used, for the most part, to pat teachers on the head, but in many states it has transformed into a way to differentiate pay, responsibility, and tenure. Principals are now called upon to evaluate teachers according to the district protocols, state requirements, and union agreements.

What you need to keep on paper as it relates to teacher evaluations can be summed up in one word: proof. Proof that a preconference occurred. Proof of when the principal entered and exited the classroom. Proof that the post-conference occurred. Once again, documentation is your friend.

However, how do you gather such proof without constantly asking for signatures, which does not necessarily elicit trust? Documentation does not need to be affirmed by others. You can go back to your appointment book, composition book, or legal pad and document the date and the time of, for example, a preconference. You can document entrance and exit requirements for the observation, and have teachers sign to affirm they have received feedback. Position yourself so you can always prove what you did, when you did it, and how you did it. And make sure you have backups of your documentation. If you record your information on paper, we recommend scanning and saving the documents. If you record your information electronically, make sure to back it up.

LOW-PERFORMING EMPLOYEES

The documentation process for low-performing employees can sometimes be laborious and time-consuming; however, addressing low-performing employees is paramount to making student achievement happen.

Documentation of performance issues begins with your daily personal documentation system (see section entitled "How to Documen"). A questionable situation that does not warrant a written reprimand in September may be the beginning of a pattern that is evident by December. It will be difficult to call something a pattern without the accompanying documentation that shows the problem has existed for a period of time.

In addition, it is not fair, or best practice, to merely *document* poor performance. You need to discuss the issue with the teacher. In many cases, the discussion will be enough to change the teacher's actions. These difficult conversations can be a challenge, especially for principals who are conflict-averse. However, they are critical. Whatever interventions and assistance you implement, document them, too. You need to be able to show that you talked with the teacher; made suggestions; offered additional training, observations, or mentoring; or recommended professional literature designed to improve the employee's performance. In sum, you need to document what was wrong with the employee's performance, what you did to try to improve the performance, and what happened as a result.

Different organizations have formal processes for documenting performance and dealing with low performance. Those organizations may or may not have required forms or documentation structures. If your district doesn't provide forms or templates, we highly recommend creating your own template. When doing so, remember that you are providing support to address a teacher's deficiency, not just documenting the deficiency. On your template, include spaces to detail the initial reason for the assistance; the steps planned to help the teacher improve; and the expected timeline for the teacher to rectify the deficiency. These details provide transparency for you and clear expectations for the employee. The template can also help ensure consistency if multiple administrators work with teachers on their deficiencies.

In addition to the template for the initial plan, create another template to document the follow-up meetings and actions that you and the teacher have taken. Sometimes at the beginning of the process, the teacher might be hostile or defensive in these meetings. In such circumstances, the teacher might want to record the conversation. Do not object to this recording, but you should also record the conversation if the employee does. This action provides you with a copy and can be easily accomplished with today's cell phones. You will want an audio copy for your own records in case the employee files a grievance regarding something that was said during one of these meetings. Or, in the case of dismissal, the employee denies these meetings ever took place and fails to produce his or her own recording. In addition, always maintain your own recording in case the teacher's version has been edited or compromised.

Depending on your district or state regulations or union agreements, your files regarding employee performance may not be private. In Tennessee, anyone can look at an employee's file. Even if you are allowed to keep private files, it doesn't mean you should. Once again, transparency is at the heart of trust, and all employees want and deserve to be able to trust their principal. Assuming all files are open to everyone will also keep you from making unprofessional decisions. This is why it is so important to document without judgment, because at some point, the errant employee may be entitled to review the documentation. It is also important to remember that consistency within employee reviews exists to protect you. You may need to demonstrate that you are not "picking on" the teacher in question and show that you supervise and evaluate all employees similarly.

***

Effectively documenting the steps and decisions you make will help you plan from year to year; assist you in recalling a decision, detail, or conversation from the past; and communicate your actions and decisions to the school stakeholders. In addition to learning the legal requirements of a principal, the ability to document conversations, decisions, and actions will help you become an effective leader and handle the responsibilities of the job.

CHAPTER NINE

Speaking the Different Languages of the Principal

The demands on a principal are almost too numerous to mention. You are the instructional leader, human resources manager, lead teacher, curriculum specialist, building engineer, facilities manager, evaluator of employees, chief parent, disciplinarian of students, parent liaison, director of traffic, transportation manager, food service director, testing coordinator, chief financial officer, and first aid director, in addition to 100 other responsibilities that manifest themselves on any given school day.

With all these demands and responsibilities, you have to speak many languages to communicate effectively with all the stakeholders attached to the demands of those areas. It's important that your message be tailored to its audience. Principals who fail to do this do so at their own peril. Messages not delivered well risk becoming messages not understood, and what may begin as an innocent change can quickly turn into a crisis.

Stories from the Field

An assistant high school principal was promoted to replace her veteran boss, who was removed for financial wrongdoing. The new principal did not live in her school's community, but she was already familiar with the pitfalls and problems that existed within the school. She began making immediate changes, which resulted in improvements. For example, it had been a tradition in this high school for seniors not to be given writing assignments because the state assessed writing in eleventh grade. The novice principal thought this hurt students because seniors needed to write for college essays and job applications, so she reinstated writing. But this was seen as a unilateral decision by families and students, who regarded it as a punishment, especially because she did not discuss it with stakeholders before instituting it.

A year later, the college acceptance rate had increased, and so had the number (and dollar amount) of scholarships granted to graduating seniors. The principal believed that these results spoke for themselves and would help convince detractors—mainly students and parents of new seniors. When she spoke with students, parents, teachers, and district officials, she explained to all of them that the data had improved.

The superintendent was pleased and held her actions as a model for school turnaround. Parents, on the other hand—whose children complained of losing a "privilege" through no fault of their own—were not pleased and found her talk about their students' quality of writing to be patronizing. The principal compared the students to students in wealthier sections of the school district, which parents considered unfair, she used educational jargon in her explanations, and she never addressed the fact that students saw the change as a punishment. The parents loudly protested what they considered to be an injustice, and despite the principal's efforts to explain her rationale, parents saw her as someone who was trying to "fix" a community she did not live in when nothing was wrong to begin with.

The principal's mistake was that she did not explain things differently to different groups. While the core message would be the same for all stakeholders, using educational jargon, research, and statistics is generally not the best way to explain to a student or parent the importance of writing.

New principals often make mistakes like this. With experience and reflection, many learn to tailor their message to the group they're speaking with. Consider what is important to that group as well as the group's background knowledge about the topic, including their existing biases and education experiences. Speaking with teachers is different from speaking with district administrators, which is different from speaking with parents, students, and alumni. People in the community such as the police, neighborhood businesses, homeowners, realtors, and the media all warrant a communication system tailored for them—even though the core message remains the same.

Being Accessible—by Text Message

One of the first things a principal has to figure out is how to develop a connection with the student body when there are so many of them and only one of you. You got into education to help and work with students, not to become some disembodied voice on the intercom. Students need to know that you care about their well-being, but this is more difficult for you to accomplish than it is for teachers, who have smaller groups of students that they spend a greater amount of time with.

Some ways to get time with students include going into each English class (or another class that every student has) and listening to the students' concerns, attending various club meetings and team practices, and interacting with students at afterschool events. These are useful ways to interact with students, but talking with groups of kids does not allow you to connect with kids individually. Some principals have a principal advisory committee, but even if you meet with 10 kids each day, it could take all year to have one exchange with each student, depending on the size of your student body—and even then you might miss some.

Texting is a preferred method of communication for most teenagers. They like the immediate response and ability to communicate without talking. While some spoken conversations with adolescents are strained, exchanges via text message typically flow with ease. So we recommend the adage, "When in Rome, do as the Romans do." If texting is how teens communicate, you may need to communicate with them this way. We recommend getting a separate phone from your personal one especially for this purpose.

Finding the Time

Many adults worry that texting with students will take up too much time. But texting is quicker than a phone call, an email, or a meeting, and if you did not text a particular message, you most likely would still need to find a way to share that information—or deal with the issues that come from a lack of communication. For instance, a student sends a picture of clothes on a rack that she would like to wear to school, but she is not sure if it meets the dress code requirements. In a matter of seconds, you can reply yes or no. If the answer is no, then you just saved yourself, or one of your assistant principals, the time of administering the punishment for breaking dress code.

Since this method is faster, it is not another thing to do; it is a smarter thing to do. Texting students is an easy way to communicate with a large student body in a personal, individual way and has been highly effective in the 1,700-student high school where we work.

Getting the Word Out

How do you implement such an aggressive communications strategy? It can start as many initiatives do, with a small group over the summer. Over the summer you can meet with groups of students who are at school for various activities, such as the student council, football team, and band. Meet with these students and communicate the texting initiative and how it relates to your goals for the year. You can ask students to take out their cell phones and add you to their contacts. Do not be surprised to hear disbelief from the crowd. Texting with the principal is unconventional, and many teens don't text with adults at all. But students will be intrigued with the idea of having nearly 24-hour access to the principal.

Immediately, the text messages will begin coming in, and word of your sharing your cell phone number for text messaging will spread through the school community. It is important to immediately respond to these texts so students know that you're serious in your desire to communicate directly with them. When the rest of the students return for the beginning of the year and you meet with them to go over the rules, expectations, and procedures, use that time to reinforce how important it is to hear student voices, and to give out your number to those students who hadn't gotten it over the summer.

Topics

The topics students will text you about are as varied as the students themselves. You may get questions about policies and procedures, suggestions for things students want to do, concerns about grades, and more. Occasionally you will learn about serious issues. For example, school holidays can be a problem for adolescents in crisis. What happens if school is out for a holiday and a student texts you that a friend has been "thrown out of her house by her parents"?

Because of this text, you can (and must) provide assistance and support. You can get the student in touch with resources to help find clothing, health care, a place to stay, and so on. In addition, students can text you to share a rumor they heard about a disruption that is planned. These warnings can help you prevent issues from arising or quickly contain them.

Although an occasional complaint about a teacher will come in, you will likely get far more "my teacher really helped me" messages from students. Many students will text to praise you for improvements to the school and thank you for dances, pep rallies, spirit days, and other things.

It is a challenge to feel close to students as the principal of a large school; however, texting with students promotes a relationship. When students come up and say, "I am the one who texted you about so and so," ask them if you texted back. (Of course you did.) When they smile and respond affirmatively, you've built a bond, and the students feel more connected to you and the school.

Anonymity

With hundreds or thousands of students texting, there is no way you can keep up with who owns which number, and you shouldn't try. Don't enter student names into your contacts, so they are anonymous. When students text with an important concern that you need to address, then you can reply and ask them to identify themselves so you can help them. Students can then be referred to other resources for depression, pregnancy, homelessness, family lacking basic necessities, or whatever the issue is. You will find that students won't refuse to identify themselves when they know you are trying to help them.

The trust that texting creates between you and students can be significant because students know if they ask for help, they will get it. Also, by only asking who students are when it's necessary to help them, you also build trust with the students that you are not trying to pry too much into their lives or go out of your way to punish them. If a student sends a text that states, "I hate dress code," there is no reason to find out the name of the student.

In responding to student texts, always let your rule of thumb be not to text anything that cannot be published on the front page of the newspaper. As for concerns about students impersonating other students or adults, we cannot say that this will never happen, but in our experience it has not been an issue. Phone numbers can be called and, if necessary, traced to their owners, so students are wise enough not to risk it.

Impact on School Security

One benefit of texting with students is that they may be quicker to text you to let you know of a dangerous situation, such as a weapon on campus—particularly since their texts are anonymous. This can enable you to prevent a possible crisis. In addition, students who fear they may be involved in a conflict will feel an extra sense of security knowing that they can contact you at any time.

Here's another unexpected and surprisingly common positive impact of texting with students: Occasionally you'll receive a message from students who are mass texting everyone in their contacts, forgetting that you are on the list. This is particularly helpful when the message deals with violating school rules. You will sometimes get these group messages about a party after school hours or an event at someone's house, but as long as nothing illegal is mentioned in the text message, then those messages can be ignored. But if the message refers to something illegal, or if it involves the school, then it is your responsibility to react.

Creating Connections

When the final bell rings at the end of the school day, students are quick to grab their cell phones and begin using them. Some students who do not have a large social circle may not have anyone to text. Those students know that they can text you, and you will always return the text. This helps reduce the isolation that some kids feel. Very often the text messages are typical teenage banter; however, when you get to know kids on a personal level and engage in the banter with them, it reduces your feelings of isolation, too.

Teacher and Parent Response

Expect a principal texting plan to be a surprise to the teachers. They will want to be assured that students will not get mad during class, take out their phones, and demand to text you on the spot, or text you about every complaint they have about teachers. You need to assure the teachers that the rules of the classrooms still apply, and if texting during class is against the rules, it doesn't become okay just because the student is texting you. Once teachers see that you are not trying to use texting to work with students against them, they are generally supportive, and many of them will begin to text you as well.

The parents of students who text the principal are generally supportive, too. They appreciate that their children are listened to and have access to the leader of the school at any time. Many parents will also text you. They value the communication and the access that texting provides.

Communicating with Students and Parents

Students and their parents look to the principal as a benevolent leader. Gone are the days when the principal was the hated guy—out of touch with the student body, handing out detention slips to tardy students. Students and parents want a personal connection with their principal. They want the principal to know their names, celebrate their birthdays, take pleasure in their achievements, and handle student disputes in a manner that is, above all else, fair.

When communicating with students and parents, focus on how your message benefits students. Parents want their child's school to have a good reputation, be safe, and be a fun place that makes their child happy. No doubt you want these things, too, but of course the things that make students happy may not always be the best things for them or the school. If students think they'll be happy in a school with lax rules and no tests, for example, you will need to carefully communicate your initiatives and ideas through the lens of students' future happiness in order to garner support. Students will not be happy to find themselves unable to get into a college of their choice or qualify for a job that they really want. Show how a change now, such as weekly ACT prep instead of free time at the end of the lunch period, might not seem like much fun but will be better for students and parents when ACT scores increase—and their college prospects improve.

Of high importance to parents is timeliness. When you say you will call a parent back by the end of the school day, the parent will watch the clock to make sure that the call is returned. It is absolutely acceptable to call the parent back by the deadline and say, "I am still investigating, but I wanted to make sure I got back to you so you would know I have not forgotten about you." This conveys competence in a way nothing else can. Sometimes, in order to keep up with these phone calls, you may need to delegate an assistant principal or a teacher to respond. To make sure that person follows up with the parent, you might ask them to email you after they've made contact.

A major complaint parents have when they speak with educators is the prolific use of educational jargon and acronyms. Parents do not know what these phrases mean, and most have little interest in learning them. Even verbiage as common as *benchmark* is not widely understood by parents, which is why it is important to be as clear and basic as possible. You may need to explain why we take certain assessments, what percentiles mean, and how high-stakes classes impact students' grades or standing within a school.

It is important to treat parents as partners in their children's academic life and not as "older students." Do not speak to parents in the same manner as you would a student; instead, talk to them as if they are your equal in standing. You still need to explain things to them, but not in the same way you would to their child. A first grader may be told that a smiley face on his paper means he is getting enough questions right—you wouldn't ever use the word *proficiency*. Use that term with parents, but support it with an example of what that means in the school setting. *Proficiency* is a fairly common word, so defining it can seem condescending, but explaining what it means in the context of school is not condescending because terms have different connotations in different contexts.

We all have had the experience of being in school. For some people, school holds very positive memories, while for others those memories are very negative. You never know which type of experience the parent had, so remember to be respectful, clear, and accommodating.

Making Connections

Principals are judged on a wide number of factors when they join a school faculty. Parents will create initial opinions of you based on factors such as race, gender, age, religion, neighborhood, what school your children attend, where you grew up, what kind of car you drive—these things do describe you, but they are not a fair basis for judgment.

While certain laws prevent people from discriminating against others, nothing governs how they will think and feel. It's helpful to be aware that some people have preconceived ideas such as a male high school principal should be "tough" or a male shouldn't be an elementary school principal because he cannot be nurturing enough. While both of these generalizations have been proven false in schools across the world, it does not stop people from believing them—at least until they can make a judgment about the principal based on their own experience.

Stories from the Field

A middle school was struggling with achievement. Parents were complaining, and teachers cited a culture of fear and low morale. The superintendent decided to replace the principal with a first-year principal who had no middle school experience. Teachers and families raised concerns about whether this was an appropriate appointment. However, the district press release emphasized how the new principal was a member of the community and the father of two students at the school. The parents were appeased upon learning that the principal's children were in class alongside

> their own; they felt that the new principal understood them. This lessened their concerns about his being a novice with no middle school experience.

The district was wise in this situation to use the principal's status as a father to its advantage. Fair or not, he possessed an attribute that in this particular situation was helpful in easing the transition for the new principal. When principals are new to a school community, they need to develop an identity that demonstrates how they are different from (not better than) their predecessors.

Even when principals send their children to a different school or district, using the "parent card" to connect with parents is helpful. Principals who are parents can share their own parenting trials and tribulations as they communicate with parents, as in the following story.

> ## Stories from the Field
>
> A mom was meeting with a school principal to discuss problems with her son. She suspected her son was using drugs and was at the point of addiction. The principal talked her through how to discuss addiction with her child, referred her to potential services to help the child, and shared some warning signs to look

> for. Before ending the meeting, the mother said, "Your kids are so lucky to have you as a mom. They must be perfect kids." The principal laughed and replied, "My kids? We have been through psychological counseling, speech therapy, occupational therapy, psychiatrists, and more. We all struggle from time to time." The mother's face immediately relaxed, and the principal could tell the conversation had helped relieve the mother of the guilt and worry she was feeling over her son's troubles.

Sharing your own experiences as a parent helps parents feel less judged and helps you come across as more of a coach for parents. This is incredibly helpful in getting parents to accept and use the advice, suggestions, or warnings you share.

If you are not a parent, you may be seen as out of touch with families' needs and what it's like to be a parent. Similarly, if you don't live in your school's community, you may be seen as an outsider or someone who is using the school as a "stepping stone" in your career. Regardless of whether the former is relevant or the latter is true, both of these situations can become barriers to trust. You can also be judged based on race, gender, or personal affiliations. In all these cases, you will need to come up with a different way to connect with parents, demonstrate how you are different from your predecessor, and show what you have to offer. Sharing why you chose to become a principal can be a way to make connections. Sharing experiences that you have had working with students in the district or students similar to those in your school can be another.

You can also set up opportunities for parents to interact with you and see you interacting with their students. Host a picnic for seniors and their parents, or an afterschool meeting with kindergartners and their parents, at which you discuss the importance of school and your expectations for them as members of the school community. These can be positive experiences that build connection and trust. If you are being prejudged negatively, it will likely be a little more difficult for you to prove your dedication, but certainly not impossible.

Parents Who Are Also Educators

Having children of educators in school can be both a blessing and a curse. Educators understand the business of school and have a high tolerance for the nuisances that crop up, such as a child being pinched by a student with special needs or a teacher going on long-term leave and having a substitute fill in. They want to fill every teacher's wish list requests, are there early for open house, and listen attentively during parent conferences. They understand why the teacher requests toilet paper and paper towel rolls for a month, and they understand that the teacher does not see everything that occurs in a classroom. Educators tend to be responsible parents who return permission slips before the deadline and send their children to school in a warm coat. They take it seriously when their child is issued any kind of disciplinary action. They will quiz their first graders on number facts, help a sixth grader with a science project, and review a term paper before their high schooler submits it. Educators value education, and anyone who has worked with a parent who does not value it understands how important this is to the schooling process. Serving the family of an educator is usually a pleasure.

Except when it's not.

Educators also know the darker truths that often exist in a school. They know that the principal claiming, "I would put my own child in that teacher's class" may be absolutely false. They know some teachers are not effective, and worse, some don't like kids. They also know that once students slip through the cracks, it is difficult to redeem them. Educators know that the process of dropping out of school begins far before high school and can even begin in the primary grades. Educators know that teachers do not see everything, and there is a chance that a savvy child who bullies wouldn't get caught tormenting their child. Many educators know that, unfortunately, far too many children have been damaged to such an extent that they are a danger to themselves and others.

Because they understand the risks and stakes, if they detect something is not going well—for example, if they decide a teacher is incompetent or inefficient or does not like their child—they will pursue those concerns to the highest possible extent in a dogged fashion, because they know the squeaky wheel gets the oil. Again and again they may have seen that parents with power or money or influence can work the system to their advantage. Parents who are educators have something that is even more valuable than money or influence—they have insider knowledge about how the system works.

> ### Stories from the Field
>
> **The father of an elementary student was displeased with the complaints of his daughter regarding the organization of the classroom. The teacher was having classroom management problems, and the structure of the class was highly punitive and negative. Students were punished if they did not use the bathroom when told or if they asked questions of the teacher when working at their desks. The father tried to communicate with the teacher but saw no change.**

> The father, who was himself a principal at another school, decided to exercise his right to review any public employee's personnel file, which was legal in his state. He saw glowing, superficial evaluations, and no letters of reprimand or discipline indicating that the negative environment had been a pattern, or even identified.
>
> As a matter of record, the teacher received notification that the father had reviewed her personnel file. The teacher was aghast. She and the father held a meeting, and the teacher asked her principal to attend because she wanted a witness. The father was greeted by both the teacher and the principal with defensiveness at what they saw as his audacity to review the file. Although the three came to some resolution, the relationship between the teacher and the father was never more than an exchange of pleasantries from that point forward. However, the father did notice that the teacher seemed not to behave as negatively after that incident.

This father figuratively drew a line in the sand with both the teacher and principal that subtly indicated that he would be tireless in the protection of his child. Handling educator parents requires a delicate touch for this reason. A non-educator probably wouldn't know that the public could review personnel files, or might be concerned that the teacher would retaliate against the child. However, an educator knows that once a child's parent complains about a teacher, that teacher tends to make sure *t*'s are crossed and *i*'s are dotted when it comes to that parent's child to avoid an unpleasant conflict.

The principal in this scenario was just as surprised and bothered as the teacher that the parent would request the file and so wasn't much help to the teacher *or* parent. He should have explained to the teacher that the parent was within his rights to request the file and kept the focus on the issues in the classroom rather than on the file request.

In general, it is best to work *with* all parents—educators included—rather than against them. Educators do not make good enemies, but they do make loyal supporters. Hence, when a parent is right about an assertion, own up to it, discuss a plan to correct it, and implement the plan.

Stories from the Field

A kindergartner was walking in the cafeteria with his lunch plate when a second grader told him, "I am going to kill you on the bus this afternoon." The kindergartner reported it to his teacher,

> and the teacher and principal jointly called the kindergartner's mother, who was also a teacher, to share the information. The mother had an emotional response and wanted to know what the consequence was for such errant behavior. The principal explained that consequences could not be shared due to student privacy. The kindergarten teacher, trying to appeal to the mom as an educator, told her that she taught the second grader when he was in kindergarten, and he just "needs a lot of love." Instead of making the mother feel better, this set her into a panic because she understood the code the kindergarten teacher was using: The second grader's threat was not a fluke or misunderstanding—he'd had behavior issues since kindergarten.

The principal and teacher were right to contact the mother in this scenario. Where they made their error was in sharing too much information. Parents who are also educators are parents first and educators second. Don't share any information with them that you would not share with a parent who is not an educator. This is a mistake that teachers tend to make more than principals, but you will want to address it with your teachers and model appropriate behavior. You may feel more comfortable talking with educator parents than other parents because they seem to have a better understanding of the difficulties you face, but they are still parents and should not be treated the same as you would a fellow principal or teacher at another school who is not one of your parents.

Some educator parents may try to use their educator status to get more information out of you than you would give to other parents, but treat them with the same respect and share the same information as you would with any other parent.

Communicating Consequences Rather than Punishment

Disciplining students and communicating that discipline to parents is one of the least popular components of a principal's job. Sometimes parents agree with the discipline, and students confess their wrongdoing; other times, facts are in dispute, and parents do not support the discipline. Parents can sometimes feel powerless, and that can evoke a strong emotional response that makes them want to protect their child from the consequence, which undermines the school's efforts. It becomes a battle between you and the parent, and the student is transformed from the role of defendant to a front row observer of adult conflict. No one wins in this scenario, and the biggest loser is the student, who learns how to fight the system rather than how to stop the undesirable behavior.

The keys to disciplining students are:
1. Be consistent in enforcing school rules.
2. Administer consequences that are aligned with the behavior and serve to prevent future misbehavior.

Communicate to the parent and the student the rationale for a consequence as well as your concern for the well-being of the student. Be matter-of-fact about these consequences and not judgmental. Too often principals are uncomfortable confronting adults, so they rush through the explanation process without gaining consensus that the consequence is part of the teaching and learning experience. If the parents misunderstand the rationale for the consequence, then the learning is definitely going to be lost on the student. Take your time when explaining and give the reason for the consequence as well as what you hope the student will gain by experiencing it. Make it clear what the student can do to keep from receiving the consequence again. No matter what parents say, always go back to the equation: "This is what the student did that was against policy, and this is the consequence for that action." Correcting behavior is about developing the student's sense of personal responsibility, and sometimes in their effort to protect their child, parents can block that process.

> ### Stories from the Field
>
> It was homecoming at a high school, and one of the football players was driving his car in an attention-getting manner in front of the buses as students arrived in the morning. He sped up and then stopped short and spun the car multiple times in a series of dangerous maneuvers. The principal gave the student an in-school suspension for the day, causing the student to miss the festivities associated with homecoming. The athlete was still allowed to participate in that evening's game.
>
> The parents rushed to school to try to convince the principal to change his mind about the penalty. They argued that the day marked the student's "senior homecoming," and he deserved to be a part of the festivities. The principal explained that the penalty was pretty minimal considering the potential disastrous consequences of the student's behavior. Neither the principal nor the parents would relent, so the entire conversation was focused on the penalty, and the student's actual behavior and

> **need to correct the behavior was never discussed.**

In this scenario, the adults were so focused on getting their way that none of them took time to address the root problem, which was the student's reckless behavior. Therefore, the likelihood of the student's behavior being changed was very low. Changing student behavior is the reason we issue consequences. When the focus is removed from the student and his behavior, little learning occurs.

The challenge for principals is to remain calm, not get emotional in the face of conflicts, and keep what is in the best interest of the student at heart. Getting parents to buy into a consequence is often time-consuming, but a skilled principal realizes that it is in this process that consequences actually do the job they are designed to accomplish—changing student misbehavior.

Communicating with Teachers

Teachers look to their principal for leadership and support. When a principal advances a change in policy or practice, teachers evaluate the proposal not just as employees, but as professional educators. Teachers are quick to measure decisions on the "fairness" scale because they want to be able to apply initiatives to all students in a fair way. They understand, as the frontline workers, that they face the daunting challenge of implementing the decisions that impact students. They serve a diverse group of students, and they have to maneuver and manipulate policy to help all students, from the most gifted to the most challenged by special needs. Teachers want a principal who grasps that critical fact.

Since teachers have to defend policies to students and parents probably even more than you do, it is important that you make your message especially clear to them. It's also important to share how you're going to explain the message to parents and students. When discussing policy changes with teachers, explain in detail why you're making them and how they will be implemented. Of all your stakeholders, give teachers the most information and the most details. They need to know what to share, what not to share, and how to share it. Since they are the front line, give them pointers on how to discuss information and to whom to direct parents and students when they have questions.

For example, if a student who is emotionally disturbed creates a major disruption in a classroom, the consequence assigned to him may be different from that for another student. A teacher might know this information, but it shouldn't be shared with parents. However, what if a parent in the community asks questions of the teacher about something they heard about the disruption? When something like that happens, teachers should be counseled to say they do not know or that there are extenuating circumstances they cannot discuss. Or they may simply refer questions to the principal.

Or, teachers may have information about another staff member who is under investigation or on administrative leave. If asked questions about it, they need to know how to respond. It's a good idea to provide training about what issues should be directed to the principal, including employee issues, student discipline concerns, or media requests.

Communicating with the Larger Education Community

Principals, more so than teachers, have to communicate with people involved in education in the community, particularly district personnel, school board members, and other principals.

District Personnel

District personnel are typically easy to communicate with because they are fellow educators. They understand the complexities of the job and are not influenced by emotions in the way parents or students can be. The challenge in working with district administrators is that they are not at your school. The nuances and intricacies of the school climate are not evident to them. They may give what seems like a simple directive, but it could have numerous implementation problems for your school. When you raise these concerns, you might be misunderstood or seen as noncompliant or difficult to work with. This is why it is important to work regularly with district personnel and invite them to your school to help them understand the specifics that make it special.

When communicating with any district personnel, keep your direct supervisor in the loop and be aware of her preferred chain of command, whether it's explicit or implicit. For example, she may not care if you ask the head of literacy a clarifying question about a new literacy initiative without checking with her first, but she will most likely feel quite differently if you go over her head and contact the head of your district with a complaint.

Keep all communication on point and free of emotionally charged wording. When raising a concern about a district policy, instead of saying that it will be devastating to your student population, state what you're worried about and give the reasons why. Create a list of the potential impacts. Also, to make sure you won't be emotional, we recommend writing down what you plan to say before contacting the supervisor. Walk away from the writing, come back to it after a little time has passed, and read it again to check for emotionally charged or unnecessary language. This is good general advice in all of your communications, but especially those with the people who decide whether you have a job for the following year.

School Board Members

People have varied reasons for serving on their locally elected school boards. Some candidates run to gain political experience and for the opportunity to develop name recognition in the community. Others are recruited from the ranks of PTO/PTA leadership because they have school-age children in the community and a desire to give back. In recent years, some school board elections have turned into single-issue races about such topics as charter versus traditional public schools, support of or opposition to Common Core State Standards, or major changes made by the superintendent of schools and strong proponents from either side will run. These races usually garner far more attention and dollars, because there is serious corporate interest in the quality of schools and who controls or profits from them.

School board members take a varied interest in their involvement with schools. Some school board members may serve 50 schools in an urban area while others serve five in a suburban community or consolidated rural setting. In addition, school board members may have a preference for elementary school children or teens or may be more interested in the financial aspects of being a school board member and less involved in school activities, or vice versa.

It's a good idea to invite school board members to events such as back-to-school nights and awards assemblies. Setting up regular monthly meetings with your school board members, if they are willing, can also be quite beneficial. If they are not willing, share as much information as possible with them whenever you do get the chance to meet. Things to share include successes and challenges as well as what your school needs in order to advance. This information is very valuable to a school board member who may not understand the nuances of how some decisions impact teachers and students.

By meeting with the school board member, you have the opportunity to explain successes and needs, information that could be helpful when the board member is lobbying for things such as wireless technology or extra lighting in a parking lot. School board members hear many complaints, but there is more to a school than just the complaints. Schools have real needs, and the board member can often help rally the community in support of the school; however, they cannot promote what they don't know is a priority.

School board members, with their power to vote on policies and funding for initiatives, have great influence to positively impact a school district. They can bring attention to issues within a district, even if they don't have the power to affect change. They can put pressure on those who do. Respect the power of these elected officials without fearing it. Look for ways to tap into that power to help your school get the direction, funding, and support you believe it needs.

Other Principals

When a principal has a cooperative relationship with other principals who serve the same community, the quality of education is improved. For example, problems within a family often impact all of the children in that family, and they can be spread across different schools. It is helpful to be able to align resources and identify areas of need for families.

Stories from the Field

A middle school principal fielded a call from an angry mother. It was December and her daughter's coat had been stolen from her locker. The parent was frustrated and said, "With the holidays coming, I don't have enough money to buy a new coat. She was the only one of my three kids who even had a coat, and now it's gone!" The principal listened and asked the parent if she wanted help getting all three of her

> children new coats. The middle school principal called the high school principal where the two older students attended and worked with him to secure new coats for all three children.

This scenario describes a family in need, and the principals needed to communicate with each other in order to ensure that resources were aligned to meet the family's needs. Even when there isn't a problem or an emergency, staying in regular communication with principals at different levels in the same community can keep you from planning similar events for the same group of people (for example, a middle school's chili cook-off fund-raiser followed one week later by a high school basketball team's fund-raiser). It also helps you provide consistent services (such as weekend food programs, social work services, or school supply donations) and make the transition between different school levels a better experience for students and families.

Regular communication among principals not only provides these benefits to students and families, but it also helps develop a higher level of professional collegiality that makes being a principal less isolating. You can decrease isolation even more by building relationships with principals at your same tier level even if they work in a different community. Problems and experiences are common to all principals, and having peers to share those with and to go to for advice can be very helpful.

Communicating with the Local Community

Your communication with the community at large needs to be just as clear, honest, and consistent as your communication with stakeholders in your school community. Be proactive about sharing information that might affect local businesses and residents such as when you plan an event that will create a lot of traffic, cars, and parking issues in the neighborhood. Developing a contentious relationship with your neighbors will not make your job easier.

Two community groups you're likely to have more delicate relationships with include the local police and realtors.

Police Personnel

Communication with the local police is usually very limited and can sometimes be strained. Secondary schools have more opportunities for dealings with the local police than elementary schools do, because older students are more likely to have legal conflicts.

The police are focused on reducing the potential for criminal activity. Hence, they may not support a local homecoming parade with dozens of teen drivers, allowing students off campus for lunch, or even late start or early release days for professional development, because when students are out of school, the chance for juvenile crime increases. Developing relationships with the local police allows you to communicate about things that are a safety concern as well as get useful advice from the police to help plan for difficult situations. It also gives you the opportunity to reinforce that only a small percentage of young people represent the juvenile criminal population. Meaningful dialogue develops among those who are collegial and have relationships. Make a point of getting to know the local police leadership by name and having regular conversations about how to help the families in your shared community.

In dealing with police personnel about students who may be accused of a crime, consult with your school district and state and federal law about what information can be released. Students have privacy rights, and just because a police officer requests information does not mean you are allowed to release it. These situations usually occur without warning and can take you by surprise. Don't let yourself be flustered. If the police appear requesting information, it is absolutely reasonable for you to consult your supervisor at the district level to ensure that you are complying with the regulations that protect student privacy while also assisting the police in their duties.

Realtors

For many people looking to move into a new community, three things drive their decision: tax rates, crime, and quality of schools. High-quality education provides an economic benefit for communities. Though public education is free, people will pay for better educational opportunities in public education by purchasing homes in certain areas. As demand increases in an area, housing prices increase accordingly. With higher prices comes increased property taxes for the city or county government.

While parents will review websites and school materials and do a cursory review of the school's achievement data, many will rely on word of mouth about the quality of schools. Those who sell real estate—who keenly know how important school quality is because it influences purchasing decisions and can drive property values—are, in many ways, ambassadors of the school system. Effective principals can take advantage of these ambassadors by sharing school information, highlights, and awards with a list-serve of realtors and by inviting them to attend annual "VIP tours." All this can prove to be very beneficial for the realtor, the schools, and the future students whose parents value the realtor's opinion enough to purchase a home in a particular school zone.

Communicating with the Media

The 24-hour news cycle that we live in means that the media is starved for stories to fill their quotas. School stories tend to attract viewers and readers for local news outlets, and it's an unfortunate and serious reality that "if a story bleeds, it leads." In other words, controversy gets attention, and controversy about a school usually paints the school in a negative light.

Possibilities are endless, but common school stories include a student getting hurt, a teacher getting arrested, parents who are unhappy for various reasons, or students who are in trouble. You don't have to pay too close attention to your local media to see that a story about a book fair or a band concert might get the last 10 seconds of a newscast or a one-paragraph write-up on a local news website while a complaint against a school for one reason or another gets highlighted as "breaking news." In this world, you must be media savvy in order to effectively lead a school—especially a school that is maneuvering through any type of crisis (real or media-driven).

Speak for Your School

Leading a school means being the face of the school in the media. You know the media policies of the district, the legality of discussing

HR issues or releasing student names, and the importance of student privacy concerns. Therefore you should be the only official from the school who talks to the media. Teachers, and anyone without media training, can be manipulated by a skilled reporter. A teacher's comments can easily be portrayed as those of "a school official," regardless of whether the teacher was sharing the thoughts of the school or personal thoughts on the matter. Staff members must be trained not to interact with media without your presence and direction.

The focus in this section is on dealing with the media when a negative situation has occurred, but even when the media is covering a positive story, care must be taken in the planning of a visit from the media. If teachers are needed to speak on a particular topic or if a particular teacher is the focus of a positive story, work with the teacher(s) to practice what they will say. This can help them feel more comfortable in front of the camera and prevent them from making an offhand comment that could be taken the wrong way when pulled out of context. For example, a teacher may affectionately refer to her class as "little rascals" after a few knock the marker box to the floor, creating a mess, but when only those two words are pulled out and presented to an audience, the tone could look negative. Also train teachers not to use too much educational jargon, which the general public might not understand. If students are approved to be in the story, the same care should go into prepping them as well. This time taken before an interview can help ensure a better quality story about the school.

Likewise, when a crisis occurs, people do not want to hear from a public relations professional, because they are perceived as crisis managers—and you are perceived as hiding behind them. You should be the one speaking with the media, even if you have a public relations professional standing next to you.

It is easy to be completely overwhelmed when the media swarms, especially if you're a relatively new principal. However, this is one of those times when if you don't feel it, you need to fake it. Avoiding the media or refusing to comment rarely helps and does not keep the story from airing. It also can make it look like you have something to hide.

Identify Talking Points and Stick with Them

While you need to be available and honest with the media, you also need to be conservative about sharing information, because nothing is ever off the record. Take great caution to make sure that nothing you say can be taken out of context or misrepresented. A five-minute interview can be edited in a way that distorts your intent, resulting in a damning 10-second clip appearing on the news. This is why it is critical to identify talking points and stick to them throughout the entire interview.

Here are some guidelines for developing your talking points:
- Make them truthful.
- Make them straightforward, to the point, and easy to understand.
- Avoid the temptation to speculate about why something happened, especially before you have had a chance to investigate.
- Be careful not to minimize the event in a way that looks like you don't take it seriously.

Beware of Unscrupulous Journalists

While most journalists are professionals and have high ethical standards, some will do things that are dishonest or underhanded to get attention for their story. To help keep them honest, require all reporters to check in at the office when they arrive at your school, and always escort them when they're in the school. Be clear that the only students who can be broadcast on the news or named in a newspaper article are those whose parents have given permission. Don't allow reporters to film or talk to those students whose parents haven't given permission, even though they may insist. Even for an innocent story about a book drive or teacher of the year, students cannot be filmed unless the school has written permission. In a world where custody disputes are common, it is important that the only students who are shown are ones whose parents have consented. It's possible that journalists may not see this as an important issue, so emphasize that the safety of students is your top priority and you can't jeopardize that even if the purpose is to simply take a cute picture or share a short, pleasant story about a student.

Important: When speaking with a reporter, remember that journalists have a job to do, and that is to inform—and get page views, TV viewers, or sell copies. You are never really off the record, and reporters who seem to be friendly or casual are still likely to report anything you share with them.

Stories from the Field

A television reporter came to interview the principal of a public school about parental complaints that a teacher had been inappropriately proselytizing to students about religion. The reporter and principal talked briefly for a few minutes before the on-camera interview began. The pleasantries continued once the camera began to roll, and then in a change that surprised the principal, the reporter made a melodramatic accusation that everyone in this public school was

> indoctrinating students. The shock of this shift—and betrayal by a reporter who the principal thought understood the situation—was captured and televised, making the principal look, at best, clueless.

The principal appeared clueless because the reporter had done such a good job putting her at ease and developing rapport before the interview that she was shocked at the way she was attacked on camera. Reporters often like to capture this element of surprise, because it makes for more interesting news.

Media-savvy principals can see this strategy coming and know not to let their guard down. Even more than the truth about a story, reporters are typically looking for an interesting angle, and one that is different from their competitors. Don't get caught up trying to prove guilt or innocence to a reporter—you will inevitably come across as defensive. Instead, simply state facts and talking points. You do not get to control which sound bites are used and what the context is surrounding a quote. All you can control are your words and facial expressions while being interviewed. Being mentally prepared and having good talking points will help you stay the course in these situations.

Demand Corrections to Wrong Information

In the process of trying to get lead stories reported before their competitors, news agencies sometimes report inaccuracies. Those errors will become historical fact if not corrected, and no one cares about falsehoods reported about a school more than the principal. Of particular importance is correcting information that appears on news websites, which are continually updated and increasingly are people's main news source.

If a falsehood is reported, call the news station and speak with the news director to explain the problem. In most news outlets, phones for reporting breaking news are continually manned, so the phone is your best avenue for getting the ear of the news director and getting information corrected on the news website before the next broadcast of the local news. Assume that stories on the Web will be there forever, so getting them right is a way to control the story of your school in history.

Serve Your Stakeholders First

When a media-worthy event occurs at school, whether positive or negative—but most importantly when negative—the parents, students, and district personnel should hear the story from you first. You can do this using a callout system (automatic phone calls or "robocalls") and/or an email list-serve, but the important thing is that it comes from you first—before the news reports it. If at all possible, you want to avoid sharing information in *response* to a media report, because that puts you in a defensive mode that appears suspicious. Because the media is dealing with print deadlines and a rigid news schedule, beating them to break the news will usually not be difficult, especially since the story is evolving in your school.

There will be times when a story comes out on a news channel's website or social media account before you have sent out your official message, but these tend to reach a smaller audience than the actual newscast. Try to be ahead of these forms of communication, but if you can't, at least be ahead of the larger release of the information. You can also put the information on your website or release it through your social media outlets to reach the same type of audience.

While in the midst of these difficult situations, it can sometimes feel as if one has approached Armageddon. The good news is that a school's bad news story will quickly be replaced by some other story. The memory of it will fade for the average viewer, and you will be left with the ramifications. But stories live on forever on the Internet, so it's important to do everything you can to control these stories when they come out. In this way, you'll best serve your stakeholders and yourself.

What Not to Communicate with Anyone

The principal's job is a leadership position, a management position, and—as a community leader—a political position by default. As such, you have to be careful not to use your position to advocate for that which has nothing to do with schools. For example, you are sometimes involved with elected officials at the local or state level. Some are going to be more supportive than others, since some are more concerned with school issues. Every few years, these people are up for reelection, and they may ask for your endorsement to advance their cause. While endorsing a candidate is well within your freedom of speech right, exercising that right is not always smart. If you endorse candidate A and candidate B wins, you are in a weak political position. Candidate B wants to work with supporters, and your endorsement, even if it got little attention at the time, will be remembered by candidate B.

POLITICAL AND OTHER ISSUES

It is common for principals to feel that they do not have the same free speech rights as other citizens, because they cannot easily separate their personal life from their professional. Though it may seem unfair or unfortunate, it's true that you are the round-the-clock face of your school and what you say or do will be perceived as representing the school. You do not have the luxury of privacy others have—it's one of the costs of the job. You can support a cause, for example, one side of the gun or abortion rights issues or a particular political party, but rarely will it serve you well to have that support affiliated with your name and, therefore, your school. So it's best to keep your support private and to be extra vigilant about what you post on social media.

Principals also have to carefully navigate controversial issues within the realm of education, especially when talking with parents, community members, and school staff. For example, you'll want to stay away from debates regarding testing, charter schools, and vouchers. Even topics that seem unemotional, like what kind of remediation product to purchase or which technology platform to use, can end up being highly controversial. Getting involved in these kinds of polarities can tie up an inordinate amount of your time.

Of course you will develop professional opinions about topics that matter to you. But it's always best to avoid sharing them, because it's easy for others to take your words out of context or simply misunderstand. Others may then repeat those misunderstandings, and you will not be around to defend yourself or offer clarifying statements or context. Before you know it, a misunderstanding can become a fast-moving rumor: "Mr. Mulcahy thinks that special education students should not be included in the regular classroom." It can be very difficult to set the record straight by that time.

Perhaps you feel strongly about an issue and believe that taking a stand on it is an important part of being a leader. If you are considering speaking out on an issue or taking a public stance, ask yourself these questions before doing so:

- Is your opinion on this issue in the best interest of students, and can you clearly articulate that? If the answer to this question is no, then choosing to speak out is likely the wrong decision.
- Is this topic something that you want to have you and your school associated with? Publicity about an issue can bring attention to your school that might not be in the best interest of you or your students.
- Are you prepared to deal with the negative fallout of speaking up? This is an especially important question to ask if your opinion differs from that of your superiors. Losing your job and potentially being blacklisted from getting a job in your area might be a possibility.

- Are there others who agree with you who may be encouraged to speak out when you do? Speaking out can be easier when you have allies.
- Will your speaking out potentially bring about a change? If change is possible, it might be worth speaking out.

CRITICISM OF POLICY OR DISTRICT PERSONNEL

Do not publicly criticize school board policy, district or board leadership, or your supervisors. It would seem that this would go without saying, but it can be a huge hazard for some principals. First, it is unprofessional. Second, it is harmful to maintaining effective relationships with those whose help and support you need.

It is acceptable to lobby for an adjustment to a policy because you've determined that the status quo no longer works, but be honest and forthright in explaining your rationale, and let the system work from there. Share your concerns with those who have the power to change them and not with the media or community at large. Also keep your discussion focused on the issues, not the people responsible for the issues. Working against people interferes with your time to work for students. It is a capacity issue, if nothing else. Your job involves many political minefields, and the sloppy or combative navigation of those explosive issues will interfere with your ability to effectively lead your school.

***

As principal, you are not only the educational leader of the school, but also the political leader. Choose your words carefully at all times, for what you say will not only impact your longevity as a principal, but more importantly, the followers of your school will see your words and actions as the guidelines they themselves should follow in improving student success. By being clear and honest with your words, your school community will see you as a leader who can be trusted to lead.

CHAPTER TEN

Taking Care of Yourself

You have to take care of yourself before you can take care of others.

This adage is especially true for a principal, who has so many people to care for: students, teachers, staff, community members, and supervisors, just to name a few. You probably have friends and family to spend time with, too. While it can seem almost impossible, especially in the first few years on the job, finding time to take care of yourself can make the difference between surviving the principalship or burning out.

This chapter offers strategies to help you find life balance, recharge, manage all your commitments, socialize responsibly, and keep everything in context.

Deliberately Seek Life Balance

Many new principals serve as assistant principals before their promotion. If this was true for you, you have already had to make the transition to being an administrator and trying to find the balance between work and home. Although teachers work many hours outside of the normal school day, those hours jump dramatically when you become an assistant principal, and they jump again when you're the principal.

One reason your work hours increase is because you become responsible for areas you may not have dealt with before, such as school finances and the hiring of personnel. You'll also find that you can't schedule your day as you did when you were a teacher due to parents walking in, discipline issues cropping up, and emergencies happening. Your administrative work is consistently moved to hours outside of the school day, which leaves little time to do things for yourself.

As such, you must learn to adjust your life, or you can soon find yourself completely consumed by work and suffering physically and emotionally. You cannot create more time in the day, but if you don't take care of yourself, the school will suffer, too. The art of managing time is paramount. You can achieve some balance by scheduling yourself carefully.

Some principals find that they spend less time in the halls and classrooms than they did as an assistant principal, because they are in the office more frequently in meetings, doing paperwork, and making phone calls. This can cause you to lose connection with what's happening in the school, which you don't want. Scheduling time daily to be out of the office and walking through classrooms will keep you from getting "trapped" in your office. Also, scheduling time to attend grade- or subject-level meetings with teachers will keep you in touch with your teachers outside of evaluation meetings. Try to find ways to accomplish typically office-bound tasks outside of your office. For instance, if you need to have a discussion with a teacher, instead of arranging to meet in your office, go to the teacher's room. For lunch, pack things that you can eat while walking through the halls. Consider apples, nuts, or a protein bar instead of a cookie or candy bar.

Be aware that the odd hours, eating when (and what) is convenient, and reduced physical exercise can quickly cause weight gain and poor health. It's essential that you carve out personal time to take care of yourself physically. As with scheduling times to be out of the office, we recommend scheduling time with a trainer or workout buddy in order to increase the likelihood of honoring your workout commitments. You could ride your bike to work. You could start a fitness club at your school that any members of your faculty and staff can join. You could take walks, do Zumba, play basketball, practice yoga, or do aerobics. This not only has positive health benefits, but also can help foster relationships with your faculty. Consider having walking meetings with your administrative staff if you are discussing items that are not confidential. Keeping water, a bag of carrots, or other healthful snacks in your office refrigerator can keep you from running to the vending machine or a local fast-food restaurant.

A principal being out due to health issues can greatly impact the school, its staff, students, and parents. While health concerns are at times unavoidable, a healthful diet and exercise routine will go a long way toward keeping you alert, fit, and *able* to provide leadership. The leader needs to be present to lead.

How to Recharge

With all the responsibilities you have, it can be easy to forget to do things that make you feel energized and happy. But if you don't take time for you, your work will suffer. You owe it to yourself—and your constituents!

Spend Time with Those Who Matter Most

We all need to find time for those who matter most to us. Whether those people are your partners, children, siblings, parents, extended family, or friends, these people have been with you on the journey to becoming a principal. You don't want to forget them when the real work begins.

Plan times to be together, and make the most of that time. Think about what the other people value in time spent together. Do they value having lots of time, or is quality of time more important to them? Do they have something they love to do or share with you during the time? Knowing this can help you better plan. Making dinner as a family and sharing that meal at the kitchen table can mean a lot to some people, but others might prefer to get dinner out and go to a movie instead. For that type of person, a week of making dinner together won't mean half as much as one night out on the town, so save the time during the week and instead set aside one night for the special outing. Planning ahead can make your decreased free time sweeter.

Family and friends can also be a part of your school life. Principals have to attend school events, and taking along people who matter to you can be beneficial in a number of ways: It can be quality time spent with the person in question that also fulfills your school responsibilities. Take a sports-crazed 10-year-old to a football game; bring a budding musician to a school concert. There are also perks to being the principal at these events. The 10-year-old could walk out on the field for the administrator meeting before the game or hang out with the coaches and players in the locker room. The budding musician could visit backstage before the concert starts. These little things might not seem like much, but to certain people they could become important memories. Your parents may enjoy these events, too, and appreciate seeing the work of your students. When you take a loved one to a school event, you're fulfilling your work duties while at the same time strengthening personal relationships.

This can also help you seem more down-to-earth to those at your school. Students and sometimes even teachers or staff members may think of their principal as a robot who doesn't have feelings, family, or friends. Many students, especially younger ones, are often surprised to see their principal outside of school, as if they believe you are always at school and never anywhere else. Letting others see you interact with your own children, spouse, family, or friends can help others see your more human side. If approachability is of particular concern to you, this can be especially helpful.

> ### Stories from the Field
>
> **A principal new to a school brought his nine-year-old son to school for "Take Your Child to Work Day" early in the school year. The principal had been highly focused on the business of running a school and had not had much time to interact with staff, and as a result, staff saw him as a bit distant and not very personable. Seeing him interact with his young son was an eye-opener for them. The generally straight-laced, reserved principal smiled and joked with his child**

> **and showed a kindness that the faculty had yet to see.**

In this simple act of watching parent and child together, the teachers began to see the principal in a new light. Opening up your personal life in a small way like this can do a lot in helping you establish relationships with teachers, which will also help foster relationships with parents and students.

While it's important to spend time with those who matter most to you, it's equally important to limit your time with those who don't matter as much or who drain you. Many of us have relationships that we keep in our lives simply because we always have or because we think we should, and some of these relationships can be harmful. They drain your energy, self-esteem, and time, all of which you must preserve and enhance in your new role as a leader. These are the relationships you may need to cut out of your life or allow to fade away. While ending a relationship is never easy, the busyness that comes with being principal may help with the process.

Take Time to Rest

Most of us understand the value of sleep. We tell students and even teachers to get enough rest. But often we think of ourselves as too busy to get the sleep we need. Maybe we think we are so important we can rise above that basic human need. It is very easy to fall into getting less sleep when you become a principal. When the weight of your responsibilities is pressing down and time grows tight, it might seem like an easy solution to cut down on the one thing that benefits you and you alone: sleep.

Cutting sleep might seem like an easy fix, but you need sleep to perform at a top level. You're bound to have late nights and even, when something major has happened, sleepless ones, but don't let that be your everyday routine. If you really can't get all your work accomplished without cutting into sleep on a regular basis, you need to evaluate how well you are delegating responsibilities. It's not your job to do everything yourself, but rather to make sure that everything gets done. This is an important difference.

Take Time to Do What You Enjoy

Most of us have hobbies and activities that we enjoy. If you don't have one, now is the time to find one. A hobby provides an opportunity to step away from work, clear your head, and come back focused. Like sleep, personal hobbies or activities are often dropped when time gets tight because they're important only to you and not to all of the people you're accountable to. But if they provide you with enjoyment and relaxation, doing them is time well spent. You may not have as much time for these favorite pastimes as before, but finding at least *some* time on a regular basis is a way to keep stress down and productivity up. Time away from the school building and from thinking about school provides your mind a needed break and may even help give you a new perspective when you return. Do these pastimes alone or with friends or family, whichever is best for you.

Take Time to Be Alone

Principals are rarely alone during the day, and if they are—perhaps early in the morning or late in the evening—it is often to get caught up on paperwork. But there is something to be said for quiet, reflective, or alone time. When you are constantly needed by others, your energy is drained. Taking time to be alone can be fulfilling and energizing.

Find a Mentor

Having a positive mentor cannot be overstated. Someone to help you navigate the principalship can often mean the difference between avoiding common pitfalls and walking straight into them. The practical help is invaluable, but so too is the camaraderie. Few people understand the stresses of being a principal, and talking with someone who does can help you feel grounded and less alone.

A true mentor rarely is found *for* you, but rather someone you find on your own. In seeking a mentor, look for someone who is:

- **Trustworthy.** If you cannot trust the person, you cannot take his advice or value his insight, which is the main point of having a mentor.
- **Loyal.** A mentor will be privy to information about you that your superiors might not have, and this information may not always be the most flattering. For example, you might in a fit of frustration say to your mentor, "It is like the superintendent doesn't even care about students" after a decision does not go your way. This may not be how you actually feel, but if your mentor reports this to the superintendent in order to make herself look good, you could potentially be negatively affected.
- **Straightforward.** You need someone who will "tell it like it is" and not someone who will beat around the bush or try to protect your feelings. No matter how accomplished you are as a leader, your subordinates will often be guarded in their responses when you ask for their opinions. If possible, choose a mentor who is an outsider to the school but who is still able to give you sound and clear advice.

- **Ethical.** You need someone who will lead you on the right path and support you when you have to make tough decisions.
- **Knowledgeable.** You may have a best friend or close sibling with whom you can share concerns or discuss strategies, but without knowledge of the job and its responsibilities, that person can be of limited help. One cannot understand what it's like to be a principal unless one has done it. Therefore, the best mentor for a principal is a current or recently retired principal, preferably from your own district.
- **Like-minded.** While you don't want someone who will always agree with you, you do want someone who shares similar educational beliefs. Your beliefs guide your decision making, and a mentor who values your beliefs can help you put those into practice.

Remember Why You Wanted the Job

Few of us become principals so we can attend tedious meetings or argue about which form should be used to spend federal rather than local funds, and yet—especially in the early years of the job—it can seem like these things take up more than their fair share of time. This can lead to fatigue and the overwhelming feeling that nothing you're doing is making any difference at all.

Take time to remember why you wanted to be a principal to begin with. Was it because a principal made a huge difference in your life? Was it because you wanted to help a larger number of students than you could in the classroom? Was it because as principal you can really mentor and help teachers grow?

Whatever the reason, remembering it and taking time to do it can help you keep your focus. If your purpose was to connect with kids, go sit in a classroom or help teach a lesson. If you chose the role because you want to help teachers develop their potential, have a mentoring meeting with a teacher. If your reasons are more about working with at-risk kids, spend some one-on-one time with a troubled student. Doing the things you love, and that inspired you to become a principal in the first place, can help keep you going even on the darkest of days.

Managing Your Commitments

While school may only meet eight hours a day, five days a week, and generally for only about 180 days a year, you don't stop being a principal when school hours are over. You attend events at night and on weekends, practices for sports, and performance activities. You deal with emergencies such as the school flooding, the air conditioning failing in the middle of August, or a teacher quitting in the middle of October. You often are called on to help teachers and students with major personal problems such as deaths in the family, illness, and fires. While you don't have to be (and could not possibly be) at all of these events at all times, you do have to be on call in case you are needed.

Certain events are of greater importance than others and require that you be present or deal directly with them. Others can be handled by delegates, and still others, like a soccer practice, don't require an administrative presence at all. But if there's an emergency, people need to be able to reach you. It's important that you're informed about what's going on, but it's also important to have a life that is not 100 percent controlled by school responsibilities.

To help balance all your commitments, put protocols in place to manage the flow of information and supervision. Make sure these protocols are known to all staff, especially those who are running events or coaching teams. This can be as simple as an email to the person in charge or a sheet with all relevant information distributed to all employees. These protocols will differ depending on the type of your school; the number of administrators, teachers, and students; and your particular responsibilities, but they can be good guidelines for managing your workflow.

Plan Supervision of Events

A football game with the school's main local rivals is a much larger event, requiring much more supervision, than a soccer game with a smaller school 40 miles away. The former requires an all-hands-on-deck approach; the latter could be handled by a designee, perhaps just the coach or athletic director. Rating different events and deciding on the supervision needed can help you plan your time better as well as the time of your staff.

Determine how large the event is, including spectators, when identifying how many administrators should attend. This is subject to change in some circumstances. For example, a conflict among students could occur during the school day that creates a lot of drama and tension. If the school has a football or basketball game that evening, the conflict could carry over into that event. So although the game might be considered small in terms of interest, you would be wise to schedule additional supervision. The best guiding principle is to be over-supervised rather than under-supervised.

Keep in mind that, like you, your assistant principals have a life outside of school. Best practice is to look at the school's event schedule on a quarterly basis and allow assistant principals to choose events they prefer to attend. One assistant principal may be enrolled in a graduate class on Tuesday evenings and want to sign up for Thursday events. Another might have a commitment with family every Monday and want to work Tuesdays. Giving your staff a voice about when they work very long days helps them plan ahead and work on the balance in their own lives.

Put all events in your calendar and note who is in charge. Even when you're not at an event, you should know who's in charge.

Plan Support of Events

Regardless of the quality or size of any particular program at your school, they all deserve to feel valued and supported by the administration. While the soccer game mentioned earlier might not require your attendance, putting in an appearance would let the coaches and players know that you support them. You won't be able to attend every event, but you can make strategic plans to attend a wide variety, making your presence feel widespread.

Be deliberate about your behavior at such events as well. If you attend the talent show, taking pictures or talking with each of the different performers, regardless of age or quality of performance, can go a long way with students and their parents. Taking time to acknowledge students who helped organize an event and those in attendance is just as important to making your time count.

Plan Communication

The score of a basketball game is not pressing information, but the fact that a student in that game was injured and taken to the hospital is. Ensure that your subordinates know the best way to reach you in the event of an emergency or if there's other vital information you need to know. Provide guidelines for what is vital to you, but let your staff know that it is better to over-share rather than under-share. That way you're less likely to be blindsided later.

Items that might require principal notification are:
- Injury to anyone at an event that requires an emergency room visit
- Player or coach ejected from a game
- Parent ejected from a game
- Physical fight between spectators or participants
- Any issue that requires 911 notification

Plan for When You Can't Be Reached

Sometimes you cannot be on call, for example, if you're on a plane or dealing with your own personal emergency. For those times, establish a designee who can be trusted to make the decisions you most likely would make.

If for some reason you have to be out of the building on a regular basis or gone for any extended amount of time, your choice of a designee is even more important. This will typically be an assistant principal, and we recommend against always choosing the same person if you have many assistant principals. Out of a team of four assistant principals, two might have more experience and seem like a better fit to be designee; however, even first-year assistant principals deserve opportunities to gain experience. If you choose only the most experienced assistant principals for this job every time, you are continuing the gap of knowledge that exists among your team.

In a school without an assistant principal, most principals choose a few teachers who share the duty of being principal designee. Keep in mind that having only one teacher as designee creates the same limited experience as having only one assistant principal serve as designee. It can also be seen as a sign of favoritism, which can have a negative effect on faculty morale. So while you may have one or two teachers who you trust the most or who are the most reliable, try to distribute the responsibility as much as possible.

It is important that the designee follow your wishes and not decide to "be" the principal. A designee should be someone who has proven to be loyal and who generally makes decisions that are in line with what you want. After choosing the right person, it is important to specifically train the individual in how to handle a variety of situations. This includes explaining what can wait until you return and what needs to be dealt with immediately, and when to contact people outside of the building.

Leaders Don't Get Their Social Needs Met at Work

Principals are social beings like everyone else. You and your faculty work long hours together, and it's common to see your colleagues more often than your own family when you add up the hours. Occasionally, those working relationships develop into social connections, and this is where things can go wrong for a number of reasons.

Socializing Compromises Equity

No one wants their principal to have favorites. It is challenging enough to avoid teachers' perceptions or misperceptions about fairness without giving them firsthand evidence by going out socially with one teacher or a group of teachers. No principal has the time to carry on a social relationship with every employee, and to be honest, you'll probably prefer to be with one teacher over another. But if you aren't willing or able to do an activity, such as going to happy hour, with all employees, don't do it with any of them.

Socializing with the principal disturbs the power balance within schools, because once you have a social relationship with someone, others will perceive that the person has higher access to you. Even if you don't discuss work when socializing with teachers, it will be nearly impossible for other teachers to believe that. And the reality is that the activity you share with staff, such as golfing, yields social opportunities where the staff member does indeed get access that others do not. That results in some teachers having greater influence over you than others based on nothing other than common social interests.

While you may not believe anyone knows or cares who you maintain social relationships with, you can bet the faculty is watching and will use what they see as evidence of favoritism. Two issues are at play here—the compromising of equity and the appearance of compromising equity. Both can be a problem.

Socializing Compromises Confidentiality

If you're spending time with people in an atmosphere that is more relaxed than the school, that informality makes it tempting to share information you should not. It's never okay for a principal to engage in gossip about staff members. All it takes is one or two beers for people to let down their guard and say, for example, "How come Ms. O'Shea doesn't have to do afternoon bus duty?" And before you can order your next drink, you feel the need to explain that Ms. O'Shea's son is receiving inpatient addiction treatment, and she must be there for family therapy (or whatever else the reason may be). This is nobody's business but Ms. O'Shea's and yours, and it's potentially hurtful to others when you betray their personal information in a social situation. When social-professional lines get blurred, it is easy to break confidences.

It's Difficult to Supervise One's Friends

When you share a common interest with staff members, friendships can develop. This can be a satisfying arrangement until an employee's job performance suffers for some reason. That friend may not even ask for special treatment, but you're likely to feel compelled to provide it out of sympathy.

Stories from the Field

A parent was upset about preferential treatment a teacher was giving some third graders in his class. The parent cited evidence that supported this belief, and the principal arranged a meeting with the parent and teacher to discuss the

> concerns. The meeting was uneventful, and the teacher agreed to be attentive to the concerns. The parent emailed the principal and teacher after the meeting to reiterate her worries, and the principal responded saying that he would "closely monitor the situation." Upon reading that response, the teacher, who was the principal's close friend, felt that the principal was not giving him the benefit of the doubt and was even siding with the parent. This compromised both their working relationship and their personal friendship.

In this scenario, the principal was trying to reassure the parent. However, because of the close relationship with the teacher and emotion that existed between them, the teacher was hypersensitive to what would typically be considered an ordinary response.

Damage Can Be Done to a Principal's Reputation

Today's friends can become tomorrow's enemies. Misunderstandings occur, and people grow apart. Sometimes only one person in a relationship wants distance. Even in the best of circumstances, break ups can be difficult. When a staff member has knowledge of your personal life, that staff member can use it to harm you. This is why it's wise to restrict your socializing to people you don't have reporting relationships with.

The job of principal demands respect, and a professional reputation that has taken decades to build can easily be demolished with improper social relationships. No one wants to see their boss drunk or hear about their boss's highly personal problems. Part of the respect your subordinates have for you stems from the mystery that is associated with not knowing too much about your personal life.

It's Lonely Being the Principal!

If you are not going to get your social needs met at work, how do you avoid the isolation that often accompanies the job?

Many principals feel a kinship with other principals. These peer relationships can be very satisfying, particularly when you're working with a person who is similar in age, works at a school of the same grade level, or has common interests with you. It can be extremely helpful to ask a colleague how she handles certain situations and hear a response that is grounded in experience from the school down the road—a school that is operating under the same district rules and regulations.

The problem for principals, of course, is the limited time they have to develop these relationships. School activities monopolize a great deal of your time and that of your principal peers. Many have found that organizing monthly gatherings provides a needed reprieve from the stress of the job. The chance to share a meal with peers where you're not required to supervise anyone helps add humor and gain some needed perspective.

It is also possible that in a small or rural district, you may be one of only a handful of principals, or the closest principal may be a 30-minute drive away. In these cases, technology may be the answer. Networking through email, texts, or online forums with principals you have met at a conference, through mutual acquaintances, or via other means may be a way to feel a sense of connection with other principals.

The Principal Is Not a Superhero

As principal, it can be easy to get caught up in the idea that you can do no wrong and that you need to have the correct answer to everyone's problem right now. But you are not a superhero and you can't do everything perfectly all the time. And here comes a shocking piece of news: That's okay!

You will make mistakes, and that is okay! You will sometimes even need to sleep, and that is okay! You will sometimes not be sure what to do, and ... that is okay, too!

What's important is not perfection but dedication to that driving force behind all your actions and decisions—your guiding principles: Is the success and well-being of students at the heart of all you do? If so, then you are moving on the right track. It's impossible to always do everything right, but you can always do everything for the right reasons. Principals do important work. You'll always have those weeks when you wonder, when *do* I sleep? But here's something non-principals don't know: We do sleep at night. And we can sleep soundly when we know that what we are doing is good work in the interest of the students you serve.

This is the work of the principal.

REFERENCES

Anonymous. 2011. "Best Principals Espouse Collective Leadership, Research Finds." *Education Digest: Essential Readings Condensed for Quick Review.* Vol 76, no 7: 63–64.

Ärlestig, Helene. 2007. "Principals' Communication Inside Schools: A Contribution to School Improvement." *The Educational Forum.* Vol 71, no 3: 262–273.

Carter, K., and W. Doyle. 1987. "Teachers' Knowledge Structures and Comprehension Processes." In J. Calderhead (Ed.), *Exploring Teachers' Thinking.* London, Great Britain: Cassell Educational Limited.

Cooper, E.J., and J. Sherk. 1989. "Addressing Urban School Reform: Issues and Alliances." *Journal of Negro Education.* Vol 58, no 3.

Covey, Stephen R., and Keith A. Gulledge. 1994. "Principle-Centered Leadership and Change." *The Journal for Quality and Participation.* Vol 17, no 2: 12–21.

Darling-Hammond, Linda. 2000. "Teacher Quality and Student Achievement: A Review of State Policy Evidence." *Education Policy Analysis Archives.* Vol 8, no 1.

Hill, Heather C., Brian Rowan, and Deborah Loewenberg Ball. 2005. "Effects of Teachers' Mathematical Knowledge for Teacher on Student Achievement." *American Educational Research Journal.* Vol 42, no 2: 371–406.

Hoerr, Thomas R. 1996. "Collegiality: A New Way to Define Instructional Leadership." *Phi Delta Kappan.* Vol 77, no 5: 380.

Kessler, Susan Stone. 2009. "The Texting Principal." *Principal Leadership.* Vol 10, no 1: 30–32.

Owusu-Edusei, Kwame, Molly Espey, and Huiyan Lin. 2007. "Does Close Count? School Proximity, School Quality, and Residential Property Values." *Journal of Agricultural and Applied Economics.* Vol.39, no 1: 211–221.

Patterson, George. 2007. "The Role of Police Officers in Elementary and Secondary Schools: Implications for Police-School Social Work

Collaboration." *School Social Work Journal.* Vol 31, no 2: 82–99.

Range, Bret G., Susan Scherz, Carleton R. Holt, and Suzanne Young. 2011. "Supervision and Evaluation: The Wyoming Perspective." *Educational Assessment, Evaluation and Accountability.* Vol 23, Issue 3: 243–265.

Richards, Jan. 2002. "Why Teachers Resist Change (and What Principals Can Do About It)." *Principal.* Vol 81, no 4: 75–77.

Sanders, William L., and June C. Rivers. 1996. "Cumulative and Residual Effects of Teachers on Future Student Academic Achievement." *Research Progress Report.*

Sparks, Dennis. 1992. "13 Tips for Managing Change." *Education Week.* www.edweek.org/ew/articles/1992/06/10/38sparks.h11.html.

Starr, Karen. 2011. "Principals and the Politics of Resistance to Change." *Educational Management Administration & Leadership.* Vol 39, no.6: 646–660 (doi: 10.1177/1741143211416390).

Sullivan, Kathleen A., and Perry A. Zirkel. 1999. "Documentation in Teacher Evaluation: What

Does the Professional Literature Say?" *National Association of Secondary School Principals NASSP Bulletin.* Vol 83, no 607: 48–58.

Tewell, K.J. 1990. "Diagnosing the Health of Principal-Student Communications in High Schools." *Clearing House.* Vol 63, no 8: 355–358.

Wrigley, Terry. 2011. "Paradigms of School Change." *Management in Education.* Vol 25, Issue 2: 62–66 (doi: 10.1177/0892020611398929).

Kessler, Susan Stone, and April M. Snodgrass. 2014. "The House that Affirmation Builds." *Educational Leadership.* Vol 71, no 5: 60–63.

Yariv, Eliezer, and Marianne Coleman. 2005. "Managing 'Challenging' Teachers." *International Journal of Educational Management.* Vol.19, Issue 4: 330–346.

ACKNOWLEDGMENTS

Susan: Over the years I have tried to help beginning principals navigate the principalship. The job of principal is important and compelling and has created thousands of memories for me over my 21-year career in education. The notion of not having time to sleep speaks to the never-ending obligations, the phone calls to return, the emails, the complaints, the reports, the events, and the expectations—some unreasonable—that make a principal believe she must be all things to all people or else she is a failure. The reality is principals are responsible for some of the credit they receive and some of the blame, but for the overwhelming majority, principals are doing the best they can in a job that has changed dramatically over the past decade and that continues to morph as schools are led through the century. I appreciate the leaders who I have worked with and under; some of the best practice I have learned has come from their examples.

Wondering "when do I sleep?" speaks to the sacrifice that the families of principals make. The spouse of the principal often gets dragged to dances and chili cook-offs and hears the never-ending stories of life at school. I am grateful that through all the different schools I have worked, my husband Burry has embraced the events, chaperoned trips, and chauffeured our children so they could be part of "Mom's school." He has been a true partner, willfully agreeing to whatever adventure I take us on, and understanding that sharing me with my ambition is part of the price of loving me. To my children, Bradley, Zachary, and Sarah, I recognize that they have grown up in the world of school and have always heard me refer to "my kids," knowing sometimes I was referring to them and sometimes I was referring to my students. Being their mother is the most important teaching assignment of my life, and my love for them as individuals and their many talents is unconditional and continues to grow as they do. I hope that they have learned that any job worth doing is worth doing well.

During the writing of this book I lost my mother unexpectedly. Living without her has made me appreciate her role in helping me develop into who I have become. Throughout my life, my mother was quick to remind me not to get my hopes up when opportunities presented themselves so I wouldn't be disappointed. Even though I disagreed with that philosophy, ironically, I believe that wanting to steer clear of that disappointment has helped propel me to accomplish my goals.

I am grateful to my siblings Donna and Kelly for being trailblazers of life's path. As my older sisters, I listened to their stories of successes and failures at school, and I am a better educator because of them. My sister Dani has been my lifelong best friend, encouraging me, laughing at my silly jokes, and overlooking my flaws while reminding me I am strong, even in those moments I feel most weak.

I would like to acknowledge the many friends and hundreds of teachers, principals, and students who have accompanied me on my journey. They have helped me become a better leader and follower and taught me that the world's best teachers want everyone, even their principal, to learn. Finally, thank you to my coauthors, who I affectionately refer to as AS and AD, and who I have worked alongside for over a decade. I value their friendship and have become a better leader because of their counsel and support.

April: I would like to thank my husband Danny and sons Daniel and Logan, who have been so supportive as my career has always taken so much time and energy. Their support makes all that I do possible. I would also like to thank my parents Janet and Mike and my sister Michelle, who has always taken such pride in my accomplishments and been one of my biggest fans.

My life has been blessed by a series of mentors who have gotten me to where I am today for whom I will always be grateful: My father, who truly believed that I could do anything and willingly sacrificed so that I could get there. Paul Goldberg, who, when a lost teenager asked, "What should I be when I grow up?" replied quickly, "Be a teacher, of course."

His understanding of my personality and the teacher I already was helped guide my career path. Lynn Eastes, who gave that budding teacher tools and showed her what caring about students more than oneself was really all about. Bob Lawson, who brought a first-year teacher into his office and said, "You need to be a principal someday, so we need to get started on that," and proceeded to give me leadership opportunities and helped develop me as leader. Finally, Susan Kessler, who took that budding leader under her wing and allowed her to grow and finally take on the role of assistant principal, and who continues to prepare her to take on that inevitable role of principal. Thank you to Andrew Davis, who has been my colleague and sounding board for my entire career, and Brad Meyers for his camaraderie and even-headedness, and to Brad and Leslie Bryan for their willingness to help by reviewing this book.

Andrew: I would like to thank my family who has been on this amazing journey with me. My wife Jennifer and daughters Marit, Wynne, and Ellie, who drive me to help our society through improving the educational experience for all children with quality, universal public education. I would like to thank my parents Willie K. and Barbara Davis, who gave me amazing educational experiences and lit the fire of knowledge in me at a young age. To my fellow educators who I have worked with over the years in this most rewarding of second careers, thank you for showing what true professionalism, a desire to help children, and sacrifice and love looks like in an educator. To my peers and mentors, Susan Kessler and April Snodgrass: Throughout all the tears and laughter, I learned every day from you, and learned "The time is always right to do what is right."

***

Finally, thanks to Meg Bratsch, Eric Braun, and Free Spirit Publishing, who encouraged and helped us turn our presentation into a book. This process has been a meaningful professional development experience that has helped us grow individually and as a writing team.

ABOUT THE AUTHORS

Dr. Susan Stone Kessler is an award-winning educator who has spent the past 21 years working in schools with Middle Tennessee teenagers. She received her undergraduate degree, master's degree, and doctorate from Vanderbilt University and a specialist's degree from Middle Tennessee State University. She has been a teacher, assistant principal, and high school principal in two Tennessee school districts. She also serves as a consultant and conference speaker and has spoken nationally for a variety of organizations including Learning Forward (formerly the National Staff Development Council); the National Conference for Teachers of Mathematics; Association for Supervision and Curriculum Development (ASCD); National Alternative Education Association; the National Conference on Alternatives to Expulsion, Suspension, and Dropping Out of School; the National Career Academy Conference; the National Title I

Association; Rice University's Education Entrepreneurship Program; and the State of Tennessee's Beginning Principal's Academy. Dr. Kessler's articles have been published by *Principal Leadership* (NASSP) and *Educational Leadership* (ASCD). For the past 10 years, she has taught students at both the undergraduate and graduate levels. In 2011, Dr. Kessler was selected as one of three honorees for ASCD's Outstanding Young Educator Award. This national award recognizes creative and committed teachers and administrators under the age of 40 who are making a difference in the lives of children. She has also been featured as an expert in several episodes of the *Steve Harvey Show*, a daytime talk show.

Dr. Kessler is married to Eugene and the mother of three children, Bradley, Zachary, and Sarah. Visit Susan online at realschoolleaders.com and follow her on Twitter at @KesslerDr.

April M. Snodgrass is a high school assistant principal in Nashville. She has a master's in supervision and administration from Middle Tennessee State University. Her career has been focused in high school, working first as an English and theater teacher before becoming an Academy Coach working to implement the small learning community model known as the Academies of Nashville and acting as the liaison between the school and academy business partners. She has been a speaker at a variety of conferences, including the Association for Supervision and Curriculum Development (ASCD); National Alternative Education Association; the National Conference on Alternatives to Expulsion, Suspension, and Dropping Out of School; the National Career Academy Conference; and the National Title I Association. She has also been published in *Educational Leadership*. Visit April online at realschoolleaders.com.

Dr. Andrew T. Davis is currently an elementary principal and has been a teacher, coach, assistant principal, and principal in both suburban and urban settings. He earned his master's in teaching from Belmont University in 2003 and his doctorate of education in leadership and strategic change from Lipscomb University in 2013. After earning his master's, he began teaching high school English in Nashville, where he was department chair for the English department and coached the women's varsity soccer team. After five years in the classroom he left to become an assistant principal at a high school where he was the academy principal for the Health and Human Services and International Baccalaureate Academy and served as IB coordinator for one year. In the summer of 2013 he was named principal of an elementary IB World School in Nashville, a program for almost 600 students in kindergarten through fourth grade. He has spoken at a variety of conferences including the Association for Supervision and Curriculum Development (ASCD), National Alternative Education Association, and the National Conference on Alternatives to Expulsion, Suspension, and Dropping Out of School. He is married to Jennifer Davis and has three daughters, Marit, Wynne, and Ellie. Follow Andrew on Twitter at @DrAndyDavis.

More Great Books from Free Spirit

Everything a New Elementary School Teacher REALLY Needs to Know
(But Didn't Learn in College)
by Otis Kriegel

New elementary teachers, preservice teachers, and administrators.

Teaching Smarter
An Unconventional Guide to Boosting Student Success
by Patrick Kelley, M.A.

Middle school and high school teachers.
Includes digital content.

The PBIS Team Handbook
Setting Expectations and Building Positive Behavior
by Beth Baker, M.S.Ed., and Char Ryan, Ph.D.

K–12 PBIS coaches and team members, including special educators, teachers, paraprofessionals, school psychologists, social workers, counselors, administrators, parents, and other school staff members.
Includes digital content.

RTI Success
Proven Tools and Strategies for Schools and Classrooms
by Elizabeth Whitten, Ph.D., Kelli J. Esteves, Ed.D., and Alice Woodrow, Ed.D.

Teachers and administrators grades K–12.
Includes digital content.

RTI in Middle School Classrooms
Proven Tools and Strategies
by Kelli J. Esteves, Ed.D., and Elizabeth Whitten, Ph.D.

Middle school teachers and administrators.
Includes digital content.

The Common Sense Guide to the Common Core
Teacher-Tested Tools for Implementation
by Katherine McKnight, Ph.D.

K–12 teachers, administrators, district leaders, curriculum directors, coaches, PLCs, preservice teachers, university professors.
Includes digital content.

217 Fifth Avenue North • Suite 200 • Minneapolis, MN 55401-1299 toll-free 800.735.7323 • local 612.338.2068 • fax 612.337.5050 help4kids@freespirit.com • www.freespirit.com

Index

A
Absentee policies, *46, 64, 66*
Accessibility, *241, 243, 244, 246, 248*
Accommodations during testing, *95*
Accounting systems, *5*
Achievement data systems, *5*
Adaptability of teachers, assessing, *129, 131*
Administrators, *11, 12, 14*
　See also Assistant principals; School board members; Supervisor,
Alone time, *296*
Announcements, *19*
Anonymity, *244, 246*
Arrival time, *18, 19, 21, 83, 84, 86*
'Ask first' culture, *152, 154*
'Ask first, spend later' policy, *62*

Assistant principals,
　evaluation of, *204*
　keeping informed, *12*
　leadership development, *12*
　meeting with, *11, 12, 14*
　meeting with parents, *11*
　scheduling event supervision, *299, 301*
Attendance policies, *64, 66*
Awards, *108, 111, 113*

B
Bank accounts, *5*
Behaviors, priorities regarding, *12*
Beliefs and philosophies,
　about principals, *250, 251*
　communication of, *12*
　defined, *133*
　meetings discussing, *147*

of new teachers, assessing, *133, 135*
Best practices, documentation of, *221, 224, 226*
Between-class transitions, *86*
Bookkeeper, *62, 64*
Breaks during tests, *96*
Budget, *60*
Bulletin board, *4*

C

Calendars, *14, 16, 18*
Callout system, *280, 282*
Camaraderie, See Teamwork and camaraderie,
Celebrations,
  in classrooms, *96, 98, 100*
  in February, *111*
  parking during, *69*
  Stories from the Field, *98*
  for teachers, *106, 145*
Certificates,
  of appreciation, weekly, *106, 108*
  of appreciation for extra work done by teachers, *108*
  for door decorating contest, *111*
  as holiday bonus, *108, 109*
  for superlative teacher qualities, *111, 113*
Certification,
  matching with position, *14*
  of new teachers, *128, 129*
Change,
  documenting stakeholder input on, *228*
  of policies and procedures, *47, 50*
  resistance to, *184, 190, 192, 206, 208, 210, 228, 237, 239*
  Stories from the Field, *190, 192*
  veterans' responses to, *164, 166*
  See also Leading change,

Cheat sheet for district finance rules, *60, 62*
Classes,
  after standardized tests, *96*
  transition between, *21*
Classroom management support, *154*
Classroom visits, *19, 23, 113, 154, 241, 289*
Climate surveys, *30, 32*
Clothing,
  dress code, *228*
  of new teachers, *142, 143*
  of principals, *2, 4*
  of young teachers, *159, 161*
Cloud service, *221*
Commitment management, *298, 299, 301, 303, 305*
Communication, *237, 239, 241, 243, 244, 246, 248, 250, 251, 253, 255, 257, 259, 261, 262, 264, 266, 267, 269, 271, 272, 275, 276, 278, 280, 282, 283, 285*
  of 3Ps of finance, *59*
  with administrators, *11, 12, 14*
  attendance and absentee policies, *64, 66*
  of consequences not punishment, *261, 262, 264*
  of data analysis, *34*
  designated representative, *303, 305*
  with district personnel, *266, 267*
  with educator parents, *255, 257, 259, 261*
  finances, *55*
  of goals for changes, *192, 208, 210*
  grading information with parents and students, *53*
  with high fliers, *172*
  with low fliers, *180, 182*
  with media, *275, 276, 278, 280, 282*
  with mid fliers, *177*
  new teachers' skills, *143*

with other principals, *269, 271*
with parents and families, *9, 11, 248, 250, 251, 253, 255, 257, 259, 261, 262, 264*
planning of, *301, 303*
with police personnel, *271, 272*
procedures for, *9, 11*
with realtors, *272, 275*
with school board members, *267, 269*
with staff and families, *9, 11*
Stories from the Field, *237, 239, 251, 253, 257, 259, 262, 269, 278*
with students, *241, 243, 244, 246, 248, 250, 251, 253, 255, 257, 259, 261, 262, 264*
with support staff, *9, 11*
tailoring to audience, *237, 239, 241*
with teachers, *264, 266*
text messages, *241, 243, 244, 246, 248*
what not to communicate, *282, 283, 285*
young teachers' skills, *161*
Complaints, *228, 230, 255, 257, 259*
Compliance with district, state or federal rules, *64*
Composition book, *213*
Computer,
　access to programs, *5, 7*
　calendars, *14, 16, 18*
　electronic calendar, *21*
　electronic files, *217, 220, 221*
　electronic gradebook, *51, 53*
　financial tracking, *60*
　spreadsheets, *23, 60, 86*
　in your office, *4*
　See also Email communications,
Confidentiality, *305, 306*
Connections, making,
　with students and parents, *250, 251, 253, 255*
　for text messaging, *246*

Consequences,
  communicating, *261, 262, 264*
  consistency and follow through, *41*
  internal discipline matrix, *11, 12*
  for lack of grade reporting, *53*
  Stories from the Field, *262*
Consistency,
  in discipline, *41, 261*
  in evaluations, *235*
  transparency and, *192, 193*
Content knowledge, assessing, *128, 129*
Cosmetic improvements to school, *9*
Creativity of teachers, assessing, *129, 131*
Crisis team, *69, 71*
Culture, *104, 106, 108, 109, 111, 113, 115, 116, 119, 120, 122*
  'ask first', *152, 154*
  improving school culture, *37, 39, 41, 42*
  new teachers' effects on, *145*
  sharing leadership, *115, 116, 119, 120, 122*
  valuing teachers, *106, 108, 109, 111, 113, 115, 145, 164, 166, 173, 175*
  vision statement, *35, 37*
  welcoming, *104, 106, 149*

D

Daily routines, *18, 19, 21, 23*
  classroom visits, *19, 113, 154, 241, 289*
  drop-off time, *18, 19*
  evaluation cycles, *23*
  morning announcements, *19*
  regularly scheduled meetings, *19, 21*
  teacher observations and conferences, *23*
  time with students, *21, 23*
Data,
  gathering concerning the school standing, *27, 28, 30*

review school data, *30, 32, 34*
surveys to gather new, *32, 34*
teacher use of, *131, 133*
Data systems, *5, 7*
Day-to-day operational policies, *46, 79, 81, 83, 84, 86, 87, 89*
arrival at and dismissal from school, *83, 84, 86*
between-class transitions, *86*
lunch, *86, 87*
recess and playground behavior, *87, 89*
Stories from the Field, *81, 83, 84, 87*
Death,
of a staff member, *71, 73*
of a student, *69, 71*
Decision-making,
difficult short-term decisions, *39, 41, 42*
doing things for the right reason, *195*
helping students as main focus, *201, 210, 309*
shared leadership, *115, 116, 119, 120, 122, 197*
See also Leadership team,
Dedication of teachers, *133*
Delegating,
leadership development, *203, 204*
principles of, *203, 204*
Designated representative, *19, 303, 305*
Desk, *4, 5*
Diet, *289, 291*
Difficult staff, *182, 184, 186, 187, 188*
characteristics of, *182, 184*
ones known about, *184, 186, 187*
ones not known about, *187*
Stories from the Field, *186*
Disabilities, *95*
Discipline,
communicating with students and parents, *261, 262, 264*

internal discipline matrix, *11, 12*
Dismissal time, *21, 75, 83, 84, 86*
District personnel, communication with, *266, 267*
  consulting on finances, *59*
  criticism of, *285*
Documentation, *221, 223, 224, 226, 228, 230, 232, 233, 235*
  how to document, *213, 215, 217, 220, 221*
  purpose of, *212, 213*
  Stories from the Field, *215, 226, 228*
  what to document, *18, 19, 59, 60, 62, 66, 180, 182, 213, 221, 223, 224, 226, 228, 230, 232, 233, 235*
Door decorating contest, *111*
'Door knocker plan', *67*
Dress. See Clothing
Drills, *46*
Drop-off time, *18, 19, 21, 83, 84, 86*

E

Electronic calendar, *14, 16, 18, 21*
Electronic efficiency, *217, 220, 221*
Electronic gradebook, *51, 53*
Electronic journals, *217*
Elementary school, arrival and dismissal, *83, 84*
Email communications, with administrators, *14*
  positive messages for teachers, *113, 115*
  priorities, *55*
  response system, *217, 220, 221*
  thank yous for hard work, *113*
  to yourself, *217, 220*
Email list-serve, *272, 280, 282*
Emergencies and other contingencies, *46, 66, 67, 69, 71, 73, 75, 77, 79*
  children stranded at school, *73*

death of a staff member, *71, 73*
death of a student, *69, 71*
early dismissals, *75*
parent concerns or complaints, *75*
parent demands for a different teacher, *75, 77, 79*
parent disruptions and confrontations, *67, 69*
parking at school events, *69*
planned student disruptions, *67*
Stories from the Field, *71, 77, 79*
during testing, *95*
weather, imminent dangerous, *75*
Employee performance, documentation of, *221, 232, 233, 235*
evaluation cycles, *23*
evaluation of, *180, 182, 232*
Employee relations, *46, 64, 66*

See also Teacherprincipal relationship,
English language learners, *95*
Equity, *195, 305*
Evaluation cycles, *23*
Events,
See Celebrations; Emergencies and other contingencies; Parties; Pep rallies and other large student events; School events; Sporting events,
Exercise, *289, 291*
External hard drive, *221*

F

Fabulous February, *111*
Face-to-face communications, *14*
Faculty changes, *39, 41*
Faculty superlatives, *111, 113*
Failure rates, *51*
Feedback,
appropriate topics, *115, 228*

documentation of, *226, 228, 230*
employee evaluations, *232, 233, 235*
from mentoring program, *152*
from new teachers, *154*
from stakeholders, *25, 27, 28, 30*
File cabinet, *4*
Finances, *55, 57, 59, 60, 62, 64*
  'ask first, spend later' policy, *62*
  bookkeeping, *62, 64*
  cheat sheet for district rules, *60, 62*
  clarity in communication of 3Ps, *46, 55, 59*
  creating a system for handling, *60, 62*
  decision making, *197*
  district personnel consultations, *59*
  documenting, *59, 60, 62*
  familiarity with and communication about, *55*
  funding sources and spending limitations, *55, 57*
  guidelines for spending money, *57, 59, 60, 62, 64*
  mentor for, *59*
  responsibility for, *204*
  signature responsibilities, *60, 62*
  teacher input, *119, 120*
Flexibility of teachers, assessing, *129, 131*
Followers, defined, *199*
Former principal, *4, 5, 7, 9, 28*
Frequently asked questions, *149, 154*
Funding sources, *55, 57*
Fund-raising, *57*
Furniture, *5*

G

Getting started, *2, 4, 5, 7, 9, 11, 12, 14, 16, 18, 19, 21, 23*
  access to computer programs, *5, 7*

creating 'The Look', 2, 4
current staffing, 7, 9
daily routines, 18, 19, 21, 23
dress and style, 2, 4
meeting with administrators, 11, 12, 14
meeting with parents and families, 11
meeting with support staff, 9, 11
office furnishing and decorating, 4, 5
schedules and calendars, 14, 16, 18
school mini-makeover, 9
Goals, 27, 35, 37, 39, 41, 42 See also Vision and goals,
Go-to person, 152, 154, 164
Grading, 44, 50, 51, 53, 55
'acceptable' failure rates, 51
changing grades after grading cycle, 53
communicating grading information with parents and students, 53
grade representations, 50, 51
inspect what you expect, 53
number of grades during grading period, 50
single assignment guidelines, 51
submission of grades, 51
Grammar, 143
Grants, 57
Guiding principles, aligning policies and procedures with, 47, 50
communicating to administrators, 12
consistency in administration, 193
decisions should help students, 201, 210, 309
doing things for the right reason, 195

supervision of events, *301*
Gut reaction, *143, 145*

H

Hallway buddies, *66*
HAWD? (How Are We Doing?) process, *230, 232*
High fliers,
    characteristics of, *168, 170, 172, 184*
    communication with, *172*
    motivation of, *172, 173*
    Stories from the Field, *168, 170, 172, 173*
    support of, *173, 175*
High school, arrival and dismissal, *84*
Hiring new staff, *7, 9, 128, 129, 131, 133, 135, 136, 138, 140, 142, 143, 145, 166*
Hobbies and activities, *294*
Holiday bonuses, *108, 109*

I

IEP meetings, *21*
Implementation of change, *164, 206, 208*
Improvement. See Change
Incentives for full effort, *96, 119*
Inspect what you expect,
    grading, *53*
    recess and playground behavior, *87, 89*
Instructional coaches, evaluation of, *204*
Integrity of testing, *91*
Interactions,
    with administrators, *14*
    documentation of, *18, 19, 221, 223, 224*
    with stakeholders, *18, 19*
    with students, *21, 23*
    See also Meetings; Student-principal relationships; Teacher-principal relationships; Teacherstudent relationships,
Internal discipline matrix, *11, 12*
Interview questions, *136, 138, 140, 142*
Inventory systems, *7*

Isolation,
  of principals, *271, 308, 309*
  students' feelings of, *246*

J
Jargon, *147, 239, 250, 276*
Journaling, *213*

K
Keys, *4, 5*

L
Leadership,
  characteristics of leaders, *192, 193, 195, 197, 199*
  decisions should help students, *201, 210, 309*
  leader's style, *199, 201, 203*
  shared with teachers, *115, 116, 119, 120, 122*
  Stories from the Field, *199, 201*
Leadership development,
  assistant principals, *12*
  delegation promoting, *203*
  high fliers, *173, 175*
Leadership inventory, *201*
Leadership team,
  balance on, *145*
  creating vision and goals, *35*
  decision-making, *116, 119, 197*
  grading policies, *51*
  hiring new staff, *9*
  members of, *35, 116, 164, 166, 177, 187, 197, 199*
  Stories from the Field, *119, 120*
Leading change, *190, 192, 193, 195, 197, 199, 201, 203, 204, 206, 208, 210*
  character of leaders, *192, 193, 195, 197, 199*
  choosing battles, *201*
  decisions should help students, *201, 210, 309*
  delegation, *203, 204*
  implementation dip, *206, 208*
  priorities, *208, 210*
  shared leadership, *197*

Stories from the Field, *190, 192, 193, 199, 201, 208, 210, 237, 239*
Lesson plans, *64, 66*
Location for testing, *93*
Lockdown drills, *46*
Low fliers,
    characteristics of, *178, 180, 184*
    communication with, *180, 182*
    motivation of, *182*
    support of, *178, 180, 182*
Low-performing employees, *180, 182, 232, 233, 235*
Lunch,
    day-to-day operations, *86, 87*
    presence at, *21*
    testing environment, *95, 96*

M

Maintenance systems, *7*
Master calendar, *16*
Master schedule, *14, 16*
Media, *275, 276, 278, 280, 282*
    avoiding unscrupulous journalists, *278*
    demanding corrections to wrong information, *280*
    display positive in your workplace, *4*
    identifying and sticking with talking points, *276, 280*
    informing stakeholders first, *280, 282*
    speaking for your school, *275, 276*
    Stories from the Field, *278*
Meetings,
    with administrators, *11, 12, 14, 289*
    documentation of, *212, 213, 215, 226, 235*
    HAWD? process meetings, *230*
    of leadership team, *35*
    with low fliers, *182*
    with mentor, *147, 152*
    with mid fliers, *177*
    with new teachers, *147, 152*

one-on-one meetings, 21
with parents and families, *11, 28, 75, 77, 79, 253, 255*
regularly scheduled meetings, *19, 21*
with school board members, *267*
of special education and support teams, *21*
with staff, *9, 11*
with students, *21, 23*
with supervisor, *34*
with teachers, *28, 289, 298*

Mentor,
characteristics of good mentors, *296, 298*
for low fliers, *182*
meetings with, *147, 152*
for mid fliers, *177, 178*
for new teachers, *116, 145, 149, 150, 152*
for principal, *59, 296, 298*
principal as, *12*
for veteran teachers, *116*

veteran teachers as, *164*

Middle school, arrival and dismissal, *84*

Mid fliers,
characteristics of, *175, 177*
communication with, *177*
motivation of, *177*
support of, *177, 178*

Morale committee, *106, 145*

Morning announcements, *19*

N

New teachers, *124, 126, 128, 129, 131, 133, 135, 136, 138, 140, 142, 143, 145, 147, 149, 150, 152, 154*
characteristics of, *124, 126, 128*
effect on staff culture, *145*
hiring, *9, 128, 129, 131, 133, 135, 136, 138, 140, 142, 143, 145, 166*

interview questions, *136, 138, 140, 142*

qualifications to look for, *128, 129, 131, 133, 135, 136, 142, 143, 145*

Stories from the Field, *138*

support of, *147, 149, 150, 152, 154*

New-to-the-building teachers, *126, 128, 150, 154*

O

Observation notes, *113, 115*

October ooze note, *109, 111*

Office, *4, 5*

Onboarding process, *147, 149*

P

Parents,
communication with, *248, 250, 251, 253, 255, 257, 259, 261, 262, 264*

concerns or complaints, *75*

creating connections with, *250, 251, 253, 255*

demands for a different teacher, *75, 77, 79*

disruptions and confrontations, *67, 69*

educators, *255, 257, 259, 261*

expected response time, *224*

feedback from, *25, 27, 28, 30, 37*

on leadership team, *119, 120*

meeting with, *9, 11*

response to text messaging, *248*

sharing grading with, *53*

Parking,
as school events, *69*

during school hours, *84*

Parties,
in classrooms, *96, 98, 100*

parking during, *69*

Stories from the Field, *98*

for teachers, *106, 145*

Payroll printout, *7, 9*
Pep rallies and other large student events, *41, 42, 100*
Personal relationships, *291, 292, 294*
Philosophies, defined, *133*
　See also Beliefs and philosophies,
Phone, *4*
Phone calls,
　documentation, *224*
　returning, *248, 250*
Planned student disruptions, *5, 67*
Playground supervision, *53, 87, 89*
Police personnel,
　communication with, *271, 272*
　involvement in schools, *67*
Policies, practices, and procedures (3Ps), *44, 46, 47, 50, 51, 53, 55, 57, 59, 60, 62, 64, 66, 67, 69, 71, 73, 75, 77, 79, 81, 83, 84, 86, 87, 89, 91, 93, 95, 96, 98, 100, 102*
　assessment of, *46, 47, 50*
　clarity, *55*
　criticism of, *285*
　day-to-day operations, *46, 79, 81, 83, 84, 86, 87, 89*
　defined, *44*
　dropping requirements, *55*
　emergencies and other contingencies, *46, 66, 67, 69, 71, 73, 75, 77, 79*
　employee relations, *46, 64, 66*
　finances, *46, 55, 57, 59, 60, 62, 64*
　function of, *44*
　getting started, *44, 46, 47, 50*
　grading, *44, 50, 51, 53, 55*
　for morning announcements, *19*
　new teacher discussions of, *149*
　regular school events, *89, 91, 93, 95, 96, 98, 100, 102*
　teacher input, *120, 172*
Political issues, *282, 283, 285*

Positive messages, *19, 21, 23, 109, 111, 113, 115*
Practice, *44*
  See also Policies, practices, and procedures (3Ps),
Principal,
  guiding principles, *193, 195, 201, 210, 301, 309*
  isolation of, *308, 309*
  judgment of, *250, 251*
  privacy rights of, *282, 283, 285*
  reasons for becoming, *298*
  relationships with other principals, *308, 309*
  reputation of, *308*
  roles of, *237*
  transitioning from one principal to another, *4, 5, 27, 28, 237, 239, 251*
Principal, success of,
  communicating, *237, 239, 241, 243, 244, 246, 248, 250, 251, 253, 255, 257, 259, 261, 262, 264, 266, 267, 269, 271, 272, 275, 276, 278, 280, 282, 283, 285*
  culture of teamwork and camaraderie, *104, 106, 108, 109, 111, 113, 115, 116, 119, 120, 122*
  documenting, *212, 213, 215, 217, 220, 221, 223, 224, 226, 228, 230, 232, 233, 235*
  getting started, *2, 4, 5, 7, 9, 11, 12, 14, 16, 18, 19, 21, 23*
  leading change, *190, 192, 193, 195, 197, 199, 201, 203, 204, 206, 208, 210*
  policies, practices, and procedures, *44, 46, 47, 50, 51, 53, 55, 57, 59, 60, 62, 64, 66, 67, 69, 71, 73, 75, 77, 79, 81, 83, 84, 86, 87, 89, 91, 93, 95, 96, 98, 100, 102*
  self-care, *287, 289, 291, 292, 294, 296, 298, 299, 301, 303, 305, 306, 308, 309*
  teachers, supporting, *168, 170, 172, 173, 175, 177, 178, 180, 182, 184, 186, 187, 188*

teachers, working with, *124, 126, 128, 129, 131, 133, 135, 136, 138, 140, 142, 143, 145, 147, 149, 150, 152, 154, 155, 158, 159, 161, 163, 164, 166*

visions and goals, *25, 27, 28, 30, 32, 34, 35, 37, 39, 41, 42*

Principal's calendar, *16, 18*

Principles,
See Guiding principles,

Priorities for your school, *27, 28, 30, 32, 34*
getting feedback from stakeholders, *25, 27, 28, 30*
reviewing school data, *30, 32, 34*
understanding supervisor's expectations, *34*

Procedure, *44*
See also Policies, practices, and procedures (3Ps),

Professional development,
evaluating needs, *32*
for high fliers, *173, 175*
for low fliers, *182*
for mid fliers, *177, 178*

Professional interactions, *161*

Program information distribution, *147*

Progress reports, *53*

Punishment, *261, 262, 264*

Purchasing systems, *5*

R

Realtors, communication with, *272, 275*

Recess and playground behavior, *53, 87, 89*

Recharging, *291, 292, 294, 296, 298*

Reform implementation, *164, 206, 208*
See also Change; Leading change,

Regularly scheduled meetings, *19, 21*

Reporting violations during tests, *91*

Responsibility, *195, 197*

Responsiveness of teachers, assessing, *131*

Rest, *294*
Rosters, *64, 66*

S

Scanner, *221*
Schedule, *14, 16*
   for even supervision, *299, 301*
   to get feedback from stakeholders, *28*
   of meetings, *19, 21*
   test administration, *95, 96*
   work-life balance, *287, 289, 291*
School,
   determine priorities for, *27, 28, 30, 32, 34*
   mini-makeover, *9*
   See also Vision and goals,
School board members,
   communication with, *267, 269*
   criticism of, *285*
School events, *46, 89, 91, 93, 95, 96, 98, 100, 102*
   celebrations, *96, 98, 100*
   parent disruptions and confrontations, *67*
   parking, *69*
   pep rallies and other large student body events, *83*
   sporting events, *100, 102*
   supervision planning, *299, 301*
   support of, *301*
   test administration, *89, 91, 93, 95, 96*
   See also Emergencies and other contingencies,
School-provided materials, *149*
School resource officer, *67*
Secretary, *9, 11, 21*
Security,
   for testing, *91*
   text messaging's impact on, *246*
Self-care,
   commitment management, *298, 299, 301, 303, 305*

recharging, *291, 292, 294, 296, 298*
social needs fulfillment, *305, 306, 308, 309*
Stories from the Field, *292, 306*
superhero issues, *309*
work-life balance, *287, 289, 291*
Separation during testing, *93*
Set-up time, *149*
Shared leadership,
  commitment to, *226, 228*
  documentation of elements of, *221, 226, 228, 230, 232*
  general aspects of, *115, 116*
  HAWD? (How Are We Doing?) process, *230, 232*
  leading change, *197*
  stakeholder input, *228, 230*
  Stories from the Field, *226, 228*

Signatures, *59, 60, 62*
Signing folder, *60*
Sign-in or sign-out,
  rules for parents, *67, 69*
  testing materials, *91*
Single assignment guidelines, *51*
SMART goals, *35, 37*
Social functions,
  See Celebrations; Parties; Pep rallies and other large student events; Sporting events,
Social media,
  appropriate use of, *155, 158, 159*
  Stories from the Field, *158*
Social needs fulfillment, *305, 306, 308, 309*
Special education meetings, *21*
Spending limitations, *55, 57*
Spending money, *57, 59, 60, 62, 64*
Sporting events,

policies, practices, and procedures (3Ps), *100, 102*
regular school events, *100, 102*
Stories from the Field, *102*

Spreadsheet,
  of teacher observations and conferences, *23*
  for tracking duty positions, *86*
  for tracking expenditures, *60*

Staff,
  children stranded at school, *73*
  dealing with difficult members, *182, 184, 186, 187, 188*
  death of a member, *71, 73*
  evaluation of performance, *232, 233, 235*
  feedback from, *25, 27, 28, 30, 37*
  hiring new, *7, 9*
  job titles, *7, 9*
  meeting with support staff, *9, 11, 21*
  socializing with, *305, 306, 308*

Staffing, *7, 9, 128, 129, 131, 133, 135, 136, 138, 140, 142, 143, 145, 166*

Stakeholders,
  communicating with, *195, 280, 282*
  defined, *25*
  documentation of input, *228, 230*
  feedback from, *25, 27, 28, 30, 37*
  policies, practices, and procedures and, *46*
  response to change, *192*
  See also Parents; Staff; Students; Teachers,

Standard employee evaluation, *232, 233*

Standardized tests, See Test administration,

Stories from the Field, celebrations, *98*

communication, *237, 239, 251, 253, 257, 259, 262, 269, 278*
day-to-day operations, *81, 83, 84, 87*
death of a student, *71*
documenting, *215, 226, 228*
leadership team, *119, 120*
leading change, *190, 192, 193, 195, 199, 201, 208, 210, 237, 239*
parent demands for a different teacher, *77, 79*
sporting events, *102*
supporting teachers, *168, 170, 172, 173, 186*
taking care of yourself, *292, 306*
visions and goals for school, *30, 39, 41, 42*
working with teachers, *138, 158*
Student data systems, *5*
Student-principal relationships, *21, 23, 79, 241, 243, 244, 246, 248, 250, 251, 253, 255*

Students,
absences and tardiness, *86*
'acceptable' failure rate, *51*
communication with, *241, 243, 244, 246, 248, 250, 251, 253, 255, 257, 259, 261, 262, 264*
daily time with, *21, 23*
of a death, *69, 71*
discipline of, *11, 12, 261, 262, 264*
feedback from, *25, 27, 28, 30*
on leadership team, *119, 120*
number allowed in testing environment, *93*
planned disruptions, *67*
privacy rights of, *272, 275*
scheduling issues, *14*
stranded at school, *73*
teacher-student relationships, *135, 136, 161, 163*

text messaging the principal, *241, 243, 244, 246, 248*
transition during testing, *93*
Student subgroups, *30*
Style of leadership, *199, 201*
Submission of grades, *51*
Substitute teacher systems, *64, 66*
Sunshine committee, *106, 145*
Superhero issues, *309*
Supervisor,
  complaints lodged with, *228, 230*
  criticism of, *285*
  expectations for you, *34*
  financial policies, *55*
  working with, *201*
Support staff, *9, 11*
Support team meetings, *21*
Surveys,
  climate surveys, *30, 32*
  data gathering and analysis of, *32, 34*
  for documentation, *226, 228*
  HAWD? (How Are We Doing?) process, *232*
  of policies and procedures, *46*
  value of, *37*
  of views on issues, *177*

T

Talking points, *276, 280*
Tardiness, *84, 86*
Teacher observations and conferences, *23*
Teacher-principal relationships,
  assessing, *138, 140*
  social needs fulfillment, *305, 306, 308, 309*
  Stories from the Field, *138, 306*
Teachers,
  3Ps apply to all, *53*
  'acceptable' failure rates, *51*
  attendance and absences, *46, 64, 66*

communication with, *264, 266*
evaluation cycle, *23*
faculty changes, *39, 41, 42*
feedback from, *37*
mentoring program for, *116, 145, 149, 150, 152, 164, 177, 178, 182*
new to the building, *126, 128, 150, 154*
parent demands for a different, *75, 77, 79*
response to text messaging, *246, 248*
reviewing data on, *30, 32*
scheduling issues, *14*
socializing with, *305, 306, 308*
substitute teacher systems, *64, 66*
training for leadership, *120, 122*
See also High fliers; Low fliers; Mid fliers; New teachers; Veteran teachers; Young teachers,

Teachers, culture for,
 'ask first' culture, *152, 154*
 shared leadership, *115, 116, 119, 120, 122*
 valuing teachers, *106, 108, 109, 111, 113, 115, 145, 164, 166*
 welcoming, *104, 106*
Teachers, supporting, *168, 170, 172, 173, 175, 177, 178, 180, 182, 184, 186, 187, 188*
 dealing with difficult staff, *182, 184, 186, 187, 188*
 high fliers, *168, 170, 172, 173, 175*
 low fliers, *178, 180, 182*
 mid fliers, *175, 177*
 new teachers, *147, 149, 150, 152, 154*
 Stories from the Field, *168, 170, 172, 173, 186*
Teachers, working with, *124, 126, 128, 129, 131, 133, 135, 136, 138, 140, 142, 143, 145, 147, 149, 150, 152, 154, 155, 158, 159, 161, 163, 164, 166*

new teachers, *124, 126, 128, 129, 131, 133, 135, 136, 138, 140, 142, 143, 145, 147, 149, 150, 152, 154, 155*
Stories from the Field, *138, 158*
veteran teachers, *164, 166*
young teachers, *155, 158, 159, 161, 163, 164*
Teacher-student relationships, *28, 135, 136, 161, 163*
Teamwork and camaraderie, *104, 106, 108, 109, 111, 113, 115, 116, 119, 120, 122*
   culture of shared leadership, *115, 116, 119, 120, 122*
   culture of welcome, *104, 106*
   culture which values teachers, *106, 108, 109, 111, 113, 115*
   meeting with administrators, *11, 12, 14*

Test administration, *89, 91, 93, 95, 96*
   plan for classes following, *96*
   testing environment, *93, 95, 96*
   testing integrity and security, *91*
Test administrators, *93, 95*
Testing data, *32*
Text messaging,
   anonymity, *244, 246*
   creating connections, *246*
   impact on school security, *246*
   implementation of, *243*
   speed of, *241, 243*
   teacher and parent response, *246, 248*
   topics, *243, 244*
Thank yous, *113*
Title I, *57*
Tour of the school, *149*
Traffic flow, *83, 84, 102*
Training,
   of teachers for leadership, *120, 122*

of teachers on celebrations, *98*
test administrators, *95*
Transparency,
  defined, *192, 193*
  employee performance evaluations, *235*
  guidelines, *195, 203*
  Stories from the Field, *193*

V

Valentine's Day cards, *111*
Veteran teachers,
  class assignments, *39*
  as mentors, *149, 150, 164*
  responses to change, *164, 166*
  working with, *164, 166*
Vision and goals,
  defined, *25, 27*
  determining priorities for your school, *27, 28, 30, 32, 34*
  establishing your vision, *34, 35*
  goal setting, *35, 37*
  short-term decisions with long-term gains, *37, 39, 41, 42*
  Stories from the Field, *30, 39, 41, 42*
  vision statement, *35, 37*
Vision statement, *35, 37*
Vocabulary distribution, *147*
Voice mail, *224*

W

Weather, imminent dangerous, *75*
Weekly date book, *215, 217*
Work-life balance, *287, 289, 291*

Y

Young teachers, *155, 158, 159, 161, 163*
  clothing of, *159, 161*
  professional interactions and communications, *161*
  social media participation, *155, 158, 159*

Stories from the Field, *158*
student-teacher separation, *161, 163* See also New teachers,

www.ingramcontent.com/pod-product-compliance
Lightning Source LLC
Chambersburg PA
CBHW011747220426
43667CB00020B/2927